D1607746

Praise for Moods and Markets

"Peter Atwater's *Moods and Markets* offers a compelling new framework for evaluating Wall Street and Main Street sentiment and putting it to profitable use as an investor. Behavioral investing is the next frontier, and this book is an invaluable resource for those stock market operators looking to stay one step ahead."

—**Joshua Steiner**, Managing Director,
Hedgeye Risk Management

"Atwater has written a thought-provoking piece that is a 'must read' for investors of all types, institutional or individual, buy-side or sell-side. He challenges conventional thinking on what drives market performance. Atwater's years of experience in financial services combined with his critical thinking, research, and analysis have produced an insightful thesis that is also fun to read! Whether one ultimately agrees with Atwater or not, every investor will come away with new insights on the markets, an understanding of socionomics, and just maybe a changed approach to one's investing philosophies."

—**Randy Johanneck**, former Chief Risk Officer,
J.P. Morgan Private Wealth Management

"Peter's long and distinguished career in the financial services industry has made him a keen observer of how greed and fear drives markets. This engaging book offers something for everyone: for academics who have long wrestled with why financial markets are more volatile than fundamentals theoretically suggest; for policymakers who still insist that it is impossible to recognize bubbles before they burst; and for investors and risk managers who are always looking for clues as to whether to follow, or step aside from, the crowd. It provides a fresh and more complete answer to how textbook theory suggests markets behave and offers the reader an opportunity to profit from today's pervasive short-term behavior."

—**Adrian Cronje**, Chief Investment Officer and Chair,
Investment Strategy Team, Balentine LLC

"It is clear that human psychology plays a major role in the fields of economics, finance, and investments. Until reading *Moods and Markets*, I considered the most fascinating and promising fields of investing to be socioeconomics, behavioral economics, and behavioral finance. But now it may well be socionomics, which takes these concepts to an entirely new and unique level. Atwater writes a lucid, compelling, and engagingly accessible treatise on the topic, supported by many salient historical and real time examples. Most importantly, he illustrates tangible ways to identify social mood dynamics and to both minimize risk and make gains based on them. A must read for every investor and fiduciary."

> **—Michael P. Hennessy**, Cofounder and Managing Director, Investments, Morgan Creek Capital Management

"I have long been a fan of Peter Atwater since we first worked together over a decade ago and have always found his thinking insightful. Having watched market analysis evolve for more than 30 years, from fundamental to quantitative to behavioral, socionomics is the next frontier. Peter's research is meticulous, proving that 'markets measure mood—they don't make it.'"

> **—Robert Balentine**, Chairman and Chief Executive Officer, Balentine LLC

"As a long term investor in the markets, I found two aspects of *Moods and Markets* that were particularly appealing. The first is that Peter presented his material in a simple format laced with wisdom…sort of like a Buffet annual report. The second is that while I have always understood the need to buy 'fear' and sell 'greed,' I now better understand that they are emotions, while mood leads to longer term bottoms and tops that lead to longer term opportunities to buy and sell."

> **—Bob Smith**, Portfolio Manager, T Rowe Price

"Peter's insights and acumen have provided him a distinguished career and this book is no different. It distinguishes him from the herd. Peter's insights within *Moods and Markets* give you a great view into the window of investing psychology that few possess."

> **—Branden Rife**, Head of West Coast Trading, Concept Capital Markets

"Peter Atwater brilliantly provides a framework for understanding both the socioeconomic hubris that led to the great credit bubble of the past decade and the dark social-psychological hangover that has resulted from its collapse. In so doing, he offers an invaluable guide to what promises to be a very difficult and turbulent period ahead as we experience what he calls the 'me, here, and now' behavioral tendencies of the post-crash world."

—**Sherle R. Schwenninger**, Director, Economic Growth Program, New America Foundation

"Humans know mood affects their behavior. Peter Atwater opens our eyes to the power of social mood to explain economic, social, and political phenomena. The false security of models and math is unmasked. This book resets your worldview."

—**Michael Powell**, President and CEO, National Cable & Telecommunications Association, and former Chairman, FCC

"Behavioral finance meets industry practitioner. Atwater gets it because he's done it. As economic central planning chokes on its academic theories, one of the most credible sources on the business of banking tells you how it all really works, with live ammo."

—**Keith R. McCullough**, Chief Executive Officer, Hedgeye Risk Management

"There are four tenets that form the foundation of investing success: fundamental analysis, technical analysis, risk management, and mass psychology/investor sentiment. Mass psychology and investor sentiment are the least understood but increasingly important determinants of market direction, particularly at important inflection points in social mood. Peter's insightful book articulates new ways of assessing the markets from this lens and is a very useful guide to investors who are looking for an edge to enhance their portfolio returns."

—**Smita Sadana**, Founder, Sunrise Capital Management LLC

"Peter Atwater's take on behavioral economics is both unconventional and incisive. His book provides a masterful illustration of the ways in which our choices are influenced by changes in social moods and how we can profit from the mispricing in the marketplace inevitably caused by our collective irrational actions."

—**David Rosenberg**, Chief Economist and Strategist, Gluskin Sheff

"One of the great misunderstandings in the history of financial markets is that The Crash caused The Great Depression, when in reality, The Great Depression caused The Crash. Social mood and risk appetites shape financial assets; it's a subtle, but extremely critical distinction. This book is a must read for anyone who wants to understand the 'why' rather than the 'what' as we prepare ourselves with a forward and proactive lens."

> —**Todd Harrison**, Founder and CEO, Minyanville Media, Inc.

"In *Moods and Markets*, Peter gives it to us straight between the eyes— we are adrift in a sea of mood. Peter is not out to thrill us with sizzle or pizzazz; he is out to make us money and save us from embarrassment. Peter's Horizon Preference framework is the best approach I have found yet for isolating the state and direction of social mood for all of my major marketing and investment decisions; I use it all the time. I can see *Moods and Markets* on the nightstands of big thinkers around the world. With Peter's help, we can find dry ground."

> —**Bernard Del Rey**, CEO, Capital Position Ventures, and former Global Head of Marketing, Morgan Stanley Investment Management

"Noble in reason. Infinite in faculty. Investors love to imagine themselves in Hamlet's lofty terms. But, as Peter maps out in scrupulous and riveting detail, we are all slaves to the human condition. The markets we esteem as logic-driven and untainted by emotion are in fact ruled by it. His book will challenge everything you thought you knew about investing. And you will be better for it."

> —**Stephanie Pomboy**, President, MacroMavens, LLC

"If you want to understand the 'why' behind financial market performance, as well as the 'what next,' you will want to read this book. I have observed Peter Atwater at work for 25 years in the financial services industry, and the common element in his many successes is his ability to break down the complex to the simple by not thinking conventionally. He has done this again by adopting and adapting a socionomic framework to help explain market behavior and much more. This book should be read not just by executives, advisors, and investors, but also by anyone curious about the driving forces behind legislative and regulatory activity through market cycles. I have learned over the years that one ignores Peter's authentic analyses at the peril of joining the ranks of the regretful self-assured."

> —**Cam Cowan**, Partner, King & Spalding LLP

"Peter Atwater has uncovered the next 'big-macro' insight—something so big that it is almost universally ignored to the profound detriment of investors, consumers, governments, and voters. Yet it is hidden in plain sight—it merely took the right seer to fully understand social economics and present it as cogently as Peter has. *Moods and Markets* is a 'whole picture' rendering of economic activity—it adds enormously to the broader study of behavioral economics and will have enormous value to those presently charged with the countercyclical re-regulation of financial and other systemically important elements of our economies. I have observed Peter's thinking, with regard to the subject he covers in this book, develop over years. I have challenged him and debated his conclusions, having initially been skeptical. I am not only convinced of the correctness of his views, but of the monumental importance thereof to the field of economic analysis."

—**Daniel Alpert**, Managing Partner, Westwood Capital LLC, and Fellow, The Century Foundation

"I found *Moods and Markets* to be a great read. The book exposes a number of little understood truths about the role of people and emotion in areas most 'experts' try to explain solely with mathematical equations and raw data. I worked with many professionals who too confidently presumed that 'the market' had the answers. Atwater eloquently throws that into doubt. It also caused me to reconsider some strongly held truths and gives me a framework in which to do that. Anyone who wants to make better decisions in their life or work should understand how they are a part of and influenced by their 'time and place.' Reading this book will help them do just that."

—**Timothy P. Dunn**, CFA, retired global equities fund manager, Capital Research, The American Funds

"The poet John Pomfret wrote of the human cycle of life and learning when in his poem 'From Reason' he ends with 'We live and learn, but not the wiser grow.' While this is often true, what Atwater has done with this book gives us the chance to break this cycle. With his experience of deep detail from inside the finance industry, Atwater has stepped back and asked the important question of 'why.' Blending practical knowledge of the complexities of Wall Street structures with a study of human psychology, this book breaks new ground and offers a better chance of understanding the complex concept of mood—the real 'why' behind these markets we chase."

—**Rob Roy**, Chief Investment Officer, Cain Brothers Asset Management

"In *Moods and Markets,* Peter Atwater does a remarkable job of revealing to the reader the unquantifiable dynamics behind the behavior of asset classes. When the seemingly overwhelming amount of economic and financial data available in the internet age fails to adequately explain the movement of markets, the book offers the 'missing link' in an easy-to-read analysis of how our emotions affect our investment decisions and how investors migrate between 'fear' and 'greed.' *Moods and Markets* creates that 'aha' moment which brings a new level of clarity to the seemingly impenetrable web of forces shaping today's investment landscape."

—**Filippo Zucchi**, Managing Member, Zebra Fund LLC

"*Moods and Markets* should be a must read for investors, regulators, and students of financial crises. It provides an insightful roadmap on how poor decisions get made and how to avoid or minimize making such mistakes."

—**John R. Chrin**, Partner, Circle Wealth Management, LLC, and former Global Financial Services Executive-in-Residence, Lehigh University

Moods and Markets

Moods and Markets

A New Way to Invest in
Good Times and in Bad

Peter Atwater

Vice President, Publisher: Tim Moore
Associate Publisher and Director of Marketing: Amy Neidlinger
Executive Editor: Jeanne Glasser
Editorial Assistant: Pamela Boland
Operations Specialist: Jodi Kemper
Assistant Marketing Manager: Megan Graue
Cover Designer: Alan Clements
Managing Editor: Kristy Hart
Project Editor: Anne Goebel
Copy Editor: Charlotte Kughen, The Wordsmithery LLC
Proofreader: Williams Woods Publishing Services, LLC
Indexer: Lisa Stumpf
Compositor: Nonie Ratcliff
Manufacturing Buyer: Dan Uhrig

© 2013 by Peter Atwater
Publishing as FT Press
Upper Saddle River, New Jersey 07458

FT Press offers excellent discounts on this book when ordered in quantity for bulk purchases
or special sales. For more information, please contact U.S. Corporate and Government Sales,
1-800-382-3419, corpsales@pearsontechgroup.com. For sales outside the U.S., please contact
International Sales at international@pearsoned.com.

Company and product names mentioned herein are the trademarks or registered trademarks
of their respective owners.

Printed in the United States of America

First Printing July 2012

ISBN-10: 0-13-294721-8
ISBN-13: 978-0-13-294721-3

Pearson Education LTD.
Pearson Education Australia PTY, Limited.
Pearson Education Singapore, Pte. Ltd.
Pearson Education Asia, Ltd.
Pearson Education Canada, Ltd.
Pearson Educación de Mexico, S.A. de C.V.
Pearson Education—Japan
Pearson Education Malaysia, Pte. Ltd.

Library of Congress Cataloging-in-Publication Data

Atwater, Peter, 1961-
  Moods and markets : a new way to invest in good times and in bad / Peter Atwater.
     p. cm.
  ISBN 978-0-13-294721-3 (hbk. : alk. paper)
  1. Investments--Psychological aspects. 2. Speculation--Psychological aspects. 3. Business
cycles. I. Title.
  HG4515.15.A89 2013
  332.6--dc23
                              2012016000

For Janet

Contents

Acknowledgments

Although my name appears on the cover, this book is hardly the work of one person.

As I describe in my introduction, none of what I have written would have even dawned on me or been possible without Bob Prechter and Minyanville.com.

As I was researching socionomics, Bob and the teams at Elliott Wave International and the Socionomics Institute were extremely helpful both in challenging my thinking and offering ideas and assistance. I am particularly thankful for the support I received from Alan Hall, Chuck Thompson, Ben Hall, and Pete Kendall. And to Dave Allman and Bob, you both went above and beyond.

And the same is true at Minyanville Media. Over the past four years, the team there has provided incredible support to me as a contributor, and I would be remiss if I did not specifically recognize Michael Sedacca, Kevin Depew, Terry Woo, Matt Theal, Justin Rohrlich, Bill Meehan, Kevin Wassong, Lisa Caccioppoli, Lila MacLellan, Todd Harrison, and the rest of the team. Further, no recognition of Minyanville would be complete without also thanking the other "professors." Talk about a great team of contributors. And to Fil Zucchi, Branden Rife, Conor Sen, Tony Frame, John Succo, and Scott Reamer, thank you for both the support and the push back and helping me to remember that when you only have a hammer, not everything is a nail. And to Todd Harrison, thank you, my friend. Beyond being the "Six Degrees of Kevin Bacon" for the second-half of my career, you have made a huge difference in my life.

I'd also like to specifically acknowledge and thank those who generously let me include their charts in this book, particularly

David Kelly of J.P. Morgan, Daniel Edstrom of DTC Systems, Jeff Saut of Raymond James, Kevin Park of UNC, Jim Bianco of Bianco Research, Stephanie Pomboy of MacroMavens and the folks at Stockcharts, Yahoo! Finance, and CSI Data.

I am also extremely appreciative to those who took the time to meet with me and to read my ideas while my thinking was less than fully baked, particularly Clyde Haulman, Louise Kale, John Casti, Randy Johanneck, Kathleen Clem, Josh Steiner, Allyson Kaptur, Cam Cowan, Rob Roy, Sherle Schwenninger, Robert Balentine, Adrian Conje, Bob Smith, Paul Muller, Bob Newman, Tom Taylor, Craig Naylor, Don Johnson, Ed Schmidt, and the New America Foundation "roundtable." Your input was extremely helpful.

To Jeanne Glasser and Anne Goebel, of the FT Press, thank you for all of your help and support in making this book happen. You made this project a pleasure.

Finally, to family, and friends who are family, who supported me through this book-writing journey, thank you. Mom and Dad, Don and Shirley, Aunt Chris, Aubrey and Todd, Miss Lois, Suzanne, Will, and Christine, you are amazing. To Molly, Ben, and Janet, words can't begin to express how I feel—I love you to the moon and back, back, back.

About the Author

Called "one of the greats when it comes to financial services" by Herb Greenberg of CNBC, **Peter Atwater** is the President of Financial Insyghts, a consulting firm to institutional money managers, hedge funds, foundations, and endowments focused on issues facing the financial services industry and how changes in social mood affect the economy and the markets.

Peter has more than 25 years in the financial services industry, including building and leading J.P. Morgan's asset-backed securities business and serving as Treasurer of Bank One and First USA, CFO of Juniper Financial (now BarclayCard US), COO of Bank One Investment Management, and CEO of Bank One Private Client Services.

Peter is a regular contributor to Minyanville.com, and his original work on social mood and decision making has been featured by Marketwatch, NPR, the *Financial Times*, and *TIME* Magazine. His article "Gimme Shelter" on the U.S. housing market was published in the August 2011 *The Socionomist*.

Peter graduated with honors from William and Mary, where he was elected to Phi Beta Kappa.

Foreword

In April 2012, I had the pleasure of sharing the podium with Peter Atwater at the second Socionomics Summit, the Socionomics Institute's annual conference on social-mood theory. That's when I found out that we had been greatly of like mind since 2009.

Through the fog of general skepticism, individuals often contact our Socionomics Institute with excitement about the moment they finally "get it." Suddenly they are reading the news differently. They interpret events differently. They understand investment cycles. They understand history. And they no longer feel so lost about the future.

The far rarer individual, however, is one who expands our knowledge. Atwater is a life-long peak performer. After serving as a high-level officer in major corporations, he became the entrepreneur behind Financial Insyghts, an instructor at the University of Delaware, and now a leader in applied socionomics. As the second college instructor to offer a full course incorporating socionomics—an Honors Colloquium titled "Social Mood, Decision Making & Markets"—Atwater is ideally suited to fulfill his latest mission: clarifying the behavior of investment markets and, more broadly, the ups and downs of social experience.

Atwater's exposition is a passionate, informative gallop through recent social and financial history as viewed through the lens of social-mood theory. He covers aspects of the stock market, the housing market, the education bubble, building booms, mood-driven changes in accounting rules, investors' "self-assured certainty" or "self-assured uncertainty" at market turning points, and people's impulse in times of negative mood to increase certainty via nonrational actions. In doing so, Atwater helps remedy conventional views regarding the psychology of investing, the motive behind business expansion/contraction, and the role of governments' actions.

The central idea of *Moods and Markets* is the Horizon Preference Model. This idea has aged roots. When I first went to work for the Market Analysis Department at Merrill Lynch in 1975, its chief, Robert Farrell, handed me just one short book to read: *One-Way Pockets*. This insightful investigation into clients' behavior by pseudonymous stock broker Don Guyon was published nearly a full century ago, in 1917. Wondering why his clients had lost money over a multi-month stock-market cycle even though prices ended up where they had begun, Guyon pulled out all his clients' buy and sell tickets and came to a startling realization:

> *The fact that impressed me most forcibly was that the trading methods of each had undergone a pronounced and obviously unintentional change with the progress of the bull market from one stage to another. As later investigation showed this tendency to be general, it may be classed with a number of psychological phenomena that cause a great majority of speculators to do the direct opposite of what they ought to do.... The customer who three months ago had been eager to take a point profit on 100 shares of stock would not take ten points on 1,000 shares of the same stock now that it had doubled in price.*[1]

In other words, when the bull market was young, Guyon's clients saw profits as ephemeral, and when the bull market was aged, they envisioned profits extending forever. Atwater has expanded this timeless observation into a broader truism

---

[1] Don Guyon, *One-Way Pockets* (New York: Capstone Publishing Company, 1917), 16-19.

applicable to all social passions. Socionomics proposes that social mood changes are unconscious. Guyon said that investors' change of outlook was "obviously unintentional." Atwater demonstrates that people's changing time horizons are unconscious, unintentional, and often the counterproductive consequences of changing trends in social mood. He shows that when time horizons change, behavior changes. His key words—"me, here, now" versus "us, everywhere, forever"—provide excellent referents for interpreting social mood.

In 1927, Cambridge economist Arthur Pigou proposed that the macroeconomy fluctuates between extremes due to society's tendency continually to fall prey to an "error of optimism" followed by an "error of pessimism." Atwater updates Pigou by characterizing these psychological extremes as "hopeful delusion" and "fearful delusion." I agree, because people don't simply make stupid *mistakes* time and again. They repeatedly *delude* themselves and each other, because shifts in unconscious mood powerfully impel changes in levels of confidence and even in beliefs.

One of Atwater's observations is that sometimes the emotional content of media headlines expresses public mood two or three days ahead of stock market changes. This is what Johan Bollen and Huina Mao found in their breakthrough study of emotional states implied in Twitter messages. These are useful observations because we have been of the mind that the stock market expresses social mood changes within minutes or hours; but it may ultimately prove to have a bit longer lag.

Atwater goes his own way in a few areas. I have listed confidence or its lack—which probably derives from unconscious imperatives to increase sustenance and avoid risk—as one of the manifestations of positive social mood, not a synonym for it. But changes in confidence surely belong among the most important manifestations of social mood and explain many social actions that otherwise present mysteries to historians.

This book contains many nuggets that readers will want to highlight or commit to memory. My favorite chart is the one showing that the author's alma mater repeatedly engaged in major building projects right at the biggest peaks in the stock market over the past century. No doubt such timing is ubiquitous among universities, just as it is throughout the culture.

As a consultant, Atwater has a practical side from which readers can benefit. Almost anyone can make investment recommendations for a bull market. But *Moods and Markets* also gives readers a useful list of the types of enterprises that tend to be profitable in bear markets. At the end of the book, Peter brings readers up to date with an analysis of social mood at the current market juncture.

It is a pleasure to see talented writers such as John Casti (*Mood Matters*), Constantin Malik (*Ahead of Change*), and now Peter Atwater help extend and popularize the nascent field of socionomics. I hope it's the start of a long-term trend.

—**Robert Prechter** is Executive Director of the Socionomics Institute and author of *Socionomics—The Science of History and Social Prediction* (1999/2003).

Introduction

"Why," particularly in the world of investing, is a very lonely place. Most analysts and research firms are so focused on "immediately actionable" buy and sell recommendations and the onslaught of quarterly earnings that they can barely keep up with the "who," "what," and "when" of an industry. Few have time for "how," and even fewer have the energy to figure out "why."

As I looked around the financial services industry in 2007, very few analysts understood the "how" and "why" of what was about to happen. With nearly 25 years in a career in financial services, I was able to explain the "why" relatively easily. As a pioneer in asset-securitization back in the mid-1980s, I had helped companies such as Capital One, Ford, and Chrysler bundle up loans and other financial assets and sell them as securities to investors around the world. I had also worked with troubled banks, like Maryland National, during the late 1980s and early 1990s recession and saw firsthand the highly charged interplay of unprepared banking executives, regulators, the rating agencies, and investors as the credit quality of overly concentrated and illiquid loan portfolios declined. I had seen how, rather than responding thoughtfully to a crisis, those involved merely reacted to events as they unfolded. I had also been the treasurer of two major financial services firms, First USA and Bank One, so issues relating to capital, liquidity, and the rating agencies were very familiar to me. And thanks to my work in securitization and my time as a bank CFO, I understood complex bank accounting.

As I looked at the world in 2007, there was no way the subprime mortgage problem would be contained. Subprime mortgages were just the most extreme reflection of the irrational exuberance evident in the housing industry at the time. These loans were the most poorly underwritten consumer loans ever, and, as a result, they would be and were just the first to default. From my experience, I knew that credit quality always deteriorates from the peak backward. The worst loan is always the last loan made as the credit cycle peaks. Elevated losses would move naturally backward, from subprime to Alt-A and all the way back into prime mortgages. Not surprisingly, then, those investors and financial services firms closest to the eye of the housing storm would be hit first. And as it was the end of an almost 80-year price rise in housing, the magnitude of the problem would be severe.

Understanding the "why" mattered.

Awakening to Socionomics

In the spring of 2009, I was lecturing on the banking crisis at my alma mater, William and Mary, and at the conclusion of my presentation I offered that if the progression I had witnessed first in the mortgage industry and then in the financial services industry held true, country defaults would be next, with the weakest and most financially leveraged countries failing first and the financial soundness of even the strongest western governments ultimately in doubt. It was the same disease, just a different patient.[1]

Although I am sure I offered my view on western sovereign credit defaults with unequivocal confidence to the class, the reality was that I had no idea if it would be true. I was dangerously extrapolating a progression framework that had been correct twice already into something that I believed to be reasonable for the future as I saw it. Worse, I could not explain to my clients, let alone myself, why what I thought should follow necessarily would follow.

As the markets moved dramatically higher in 2009, my continued pessimistic outlook drew increasing skepticism. In the eyes of the market and my clients, western governments and central bankers had saved the day. Policymakers did what policymakers always do, they put a floor on market prices and the economy rebounded. We had learned from the mistakes of the Great Depression and an economic collapse had been averted. What could have been The Second Great Depression had been successfully mitigated to just The Great Recession.

I was wrong and would stay wrong. Even worse, I had violated a major market axiom. I had let my own need to be right get in the way of making money. Still, I had seen how much risk had been transferred from the balance sheets of private sector financial services firms and corporations onto the books of governments and central banks. From my perspective losses hadn't been eliminated, they had just been moved. I felt like the markets were celebrating the migration

---

[1] The blackboard charts I created in early 2009 ultimately formed the basis for "The Global Crisis in Nine Slides," Minyanville.com, www.minyanville.com/businessmarkets/articles/debt-crisis-fannie-freddie-LIFO-merril/2/2/2010/id/26625 (February 2, 2010).

of their losses to someone else, rather than the real end of the crisis. At every critical juncture, the monkey was merely moved onto someone else's back.

Needless to say, my wrong outlook led me to explore an endless stream of books and articles on financial history, economic theory, and investing strategies. I wanted to understand if and how banking crises tied to sovereign debt crises; and if they did tie, why.

Unfortunately nothing I read made sense to me, at least not in explaining the chronology of events and the extreme outcome that I still foresaw.

That changed in November 2009, when I saw an interview with Bob Prechter, the president of Elliott Wave International, by Kevin Depew on Minyanville.com.[2] Beginning in the summer of 2007, I had been (and still am) a contributor to Minyanville, and I often found Kevin's take on the markets to be at odds with my own. He was optimistic where I only saw gloom, and he was pessimistic when I saw opportunity. Kevin attributed a lot of his self-admitted contrarian perspective to what he had learned from Bob. And Kevin's enthusiasm ahead of his interview with Bob was palpable. He was like a guitar fan finally having the chance to sit down with Carlos Santana or Eddie Van Halen.

What I heard in Kevin's interview with Bob, though, went against everything I had learned in economics and thought I had witnessed in the markets—that social mood, something I had never before even considered as a possible causal factor, drove the direction of the markets and not the reverse—that

[2] Robert Prechter, interview by Kevin Depew, November 11, 2009, "Video: Q&A With Robert Prechter," Minyanville.com, www.minyanville.com/businessmarkets/articles/prechter-bob-depew-kevin-bears-elliott/11/11/2009/id/25382.

the S&P 500 is to social mood what a thermometer is to temperature or a barometer to air pressure. Markets measure mood, they don't in and of themselves make it.

The more I studied this, the more I agreed with Bob and the major underlying principles of the new field of socionomics. Better than anything I had seen before, socionomics explained the "why" I had been searching for.

Socionomics Defined

Socionomics is the study of how changes in social mood motivate and affect social actions and our behavior, not just in the financial markets, but across the economy, in politics, and even in popular culture. Socionomics is very different from socioeconomics, which looks at how changing economic conditions and social conditions relate. The two fields have fundamentally different views of cause and effect.

As Bob Prechter offered more than a decade ago, "Understanding socionomics requires comprehending the contrast between two postulations:

1. The standard presumption: Social mood is buffeted by economic, political and cultural trends and events. News of such events affects the social mood, which in turn affects people's penchant for investing.

2. The socionomic hypothesis: Social mood is a natural product of human interaction.... Its trends and extent determine the character of social action, including the economic, political and cultural."[3]

---

[3] Robert Prechter, "Socionomics in a Nutshell," *Elliott Wave Theorist* (November 1999): 1.

To economists, changes in social mood are a consequence of changes in the economy. To socionomists, changes in the economy are a consequence of changes in social mood.

Again, these are two fundamentally different views of cause and effect.

Moving From "Why" to "How"

While Bob and others at the Socionomics Institute helped me to see the linkages of mood to specific outcomes and consequences, I struggled with how it was that mood could actually drive them. I could not "see" the transmission mechanism. And without that I could not determine how what had happened with mortgages and banking could or even would apply to countries. This frustration led me to look more specifically at how changes in our mood affect our decision-making processes and what we believe to be logical choices across a broad spectrum of different moods. I tried to figure out why, for example, we bought homes eagerly at the peak of the market, yet with record low mortgage rates and record housing affordability, we only want to rent them today.

What follows are my findings. My goal in writing this book is to share the insights and conclusions I have come to thanks to the framework of socionomics. I hope to help investors see what I now see in the markets and in the world around us and to prosper from it. No specific understanding of or background in socionomics is at all necessary for what is ahead, nor do you need a specific background or experience in finance or investments. In fact, I expect many professional investors and traders to bristle at what I've written.

For those with a very serious interest in socionomics, I have included a bibliography of books and articles on the topic. I believe I still have more to learn; I am the first to admit that I have had the great luxury of driving down a road that Bob, Pete Kendall, Alan Hall, and others have carved out of a jungle of conflicting economic theories and investing strategies and have lain before me. Where we agree, they deserve all the credit. Where we don't, I will gladly take the blame.

What's Ahead

The first chapter of the book focuses on what social mood is, and more importantly, what it is not. Too often we associate markets with emotion, and I believe (admittedly now with costly hindsight) being able to distinguish mood and its characteristics from emotion creates an enormous advantage for investors.

I then look specifically at how mood affects the decisions we make. In that process I introduce you to something I call *Horizon Preference*, a very simple framework I developed that links what I believe are our "natural" decisions to a specific level of mood. As market tops and bottoms are of particular interest and very relevant to investors, I also look closely at those moments' consistent specific behavioral attributes.

Along the way, I do the following:

- Incorporate examples of specific mood-based decisions from different businesses and industries
- Walk through the housing bubble and the role changes in mood played there and how changes in mood are likely to affect higher education in the future

- Look at the connection between social mood and corporate accounting

I know the last section might not sound incredibly exciting, but for investors, knowing how social mood and accounting tie together is critical. Enron and WorldCom didn't happen by accident; nor did Sarbanes-Oxley.

Finally, I turn my attention to where I think we are today, and I offer where I think we are headed. To be clear up front, though, this is not one of those Dow 50,000 or Dow 5,000 books. Whether up or down from here, by the time you have finished reading this book, you should be able to make your own decision on the direction of the market by better understanding the significance of what you see in the world around you every day. To help, throughout the book I have tried to be generous with charts and sidebars that offer recent real-life examples. Hopefully, these will spur you to consider other examples from your own business or industry.

One Final Thought

Before moving on to Chapter 1, "Understanding Social Mood," though, I want to pause and put right on the table the fundamental question of "causation" and the idea that changes in mood naturally "cause" us to do things we didn't even know we were going to do.

To be perfectly clear, when I first started looking at socionomics, not only did I not believe it, I didn't want to believe it. As I offered earlier, the idea that changes in mood could move the market higher or lower ran counter to everything I thought I had witnessed in my 25 years in the financial services industry. There was no way socionomics could be right.

Today I firmly believe mood drives the market. In the chapters ahead, I explain why.

1

Understanding Social Mood

From watching CNBC or reading *The Wall Street Journal*, it would be easy to conclude that it is the economy or corporate earnings that move the market. On any given day you might hear that stocks rose on a better than expected employment figure, while on another day stocks' fall is attributed to a drop in profitability at Research in Motion or some other company.

Something had to make the market go up or down, and there are plenty of confident pundits and journalists whose job it is every day to tell us just what that specific something was.

At the risk of alienating the entire financial media complex, that something had nothing to do with today's corporate earnings or economic reports. Although they are interesting facts, what we typically attribute a market move to are much more likely to be effects rather than causes.

Instead of considering how a positive earnings report propels stock prices higher, investors would be far wiser to think about what causes an improvement in earnings and valuations in the first place. Similarly, rather than looking at how falling housing prices might be associated with falling equity markets on any given day, it would be better to consider why housing prices dropped at all.

I believe that markets are not moved by corporate or economic data or even by external events but by us; by how we feel—our mood—and, importantly, by how changes in our mood drive our preferences and in turn the specific decisions that we make every day.

Mood Defined

Before diving into the decision-making linkages to changes in mood, I first want to define what I mean by mood, particularly our collective, or social, mood. To do that, I first want to start with mood at an individual level.

At the risk of over-simplicity, I think of our own individual mood as our underlying confidence. It is how sure we feel, often unknowingly, about ourselves and the world around us. But please appreciate that confidence is an entirely forward-looking measure. Although our level of confidence at any moment exists in the present, confidence is in fact all about the future and how certain or uncertain we are, not only about what we believe is ahead (the future itself), but whether our own immediate choice of actions— our decisions—are in fact going to be successful in that future or not.

I realize that that is quite a mouthful, but confidence is all about how we see ourselves faring ahead. And only we can determine how confident we are. Others can tell us that we have too much or too little self-confidence. The reality, however, is that only we ourselves know our own confidence level. While I can try to coach a less than confident person to be more confident, I can't make him or her more confident. Confidence (or lack thereof) is ultimately determined and measured from within. Just try to convince someone you believe to be overconfident that they are overconfident and you will quickly see just how self-determined confidence really is!

Why I like "confidence" so much as a synonym for "mood" is because the word ties together what I think of as the two critical elements of mood: a measure of certainty (or lack thereof) and our own belief system—what we *think* or *feel* is right at a specific moment in time—both assessed in a forward-looking manner. And it is that forward-looking element that is vital to mood's usefulness to an investor. While our mood can and will be shaped by events from the past, it is how we apply those events to our outlook (through our hypotheses/predictions/strategies) that is critical. And as you will see, this allows us at different times to both under-and overestimate risk without necessarily realizing it. It also enables us to react differently to what is arguably the same information at different moments in time. As experienced investors know, some days markets rise on good news and on other days they fall on good news. It all depends on our level of confidence.

How Changes in Confidence Affect Our Decisions

To begin to see how changes in confidence and decision making are linked, consider your own level of confidence today versus five years ago. Are you more or less confident? Would the decisions you'd make today with regards to housing, for example, be different than they were five years ago as a function of your change in confidence level? Do you think you over- or underestimated the risks in housing five years ago? Do you think you over- or underestimate them today? Do you think home values are more or less certain today than you did five years ago? Do you think your sense of certainty in home values today is affected by your own level of confidence?

Although we don't explicitly answer such a long list of questions like this for every major purchase, our actions, are shaped by our answers and our specific level of confidence at the precise moment we act. Five years ago we would have made one decision, whereas today we might make another.

I also like the word "confidence" as a synonym for "social mood" because confidence has the same forward-looking aspect as equity values. That is to say, we value a stock today not on what is happening today within a company, but what we believe will happen in the future. I come back to this point in Chapter 2, "Horizon Preference: How Mood Affects Our Decision Making," but please consider here how naturally aligned stock values and our level of confidence are.

Mood Versus Emotion

Another reason "confidence" is a good synonym for "mood" is because it makes it clear that mood and emotion are not the same things. Being sad does not preclude me from also being confident. By the same token, being happy doesn't necessarily stop me from being uncertain. Emotions tend to be much more short term in nature than mood. Our emotions are often shaped by specific events, whereas mood tends to shape the events themselves.

Many psychologists like to link our mood to a continuum that ranges from pessimism to optimism. Although I don't necessarily disagree with the connection, I am afraid that optimism and pessimism may reflect changes in our underlying confidence/mood rather than be contributors to it. For example, I might become more pessimistic because my mood has deteriorated and I am less confident. I also feel that both optimism and pessimism carry strong links to emotion, which only makes more confusing what is already a pretty ethereal topic for most people.

With all that said, there are moments when mood and emotion are seemingly indistinguishable. Those moments tend to be at the extreme turning points of mood. (I come back to this topic in Chapters 3, "Market Peaks and All the Red Flags They Wave," and 6, "Signs of a Bottom in Social Mood"). I think this is one of the reasons why investors repeatedly make the wrong investment decisions at critical turns in the market. At the top, for example, we miss the coincidence of strong positive mood and strong positive emotions (such as joy, love, peace) because of our extreme confidence about what is ahead. Likewise, on days like 9/11 it is all but impossible for us to separate very negative emotions, such as tragedy and sadness, from an extreme level of uncertainty.

Confidence and Our Perceptions of Certainty

There is another related aspect to mood that I think is also worth considering, and that is the fact that our mood/confidence level and our certainty about the future are highly correlated. That is to say that the greater our own level of confidence, the more certain we are as to what we think the future will hold. Interestingly, too, the greater our confidence, the more into that future we think we can see our own version of that future as well. Put another way, when we are confident we think we know what is ahead, and when we are really confident we think we know what is ahead for a very long time to come. Companies, for example, routinely overinvest at the top in manufacturing capacity because they are certain of strong demand well into the future. The net result for most people resembles Figure 1.1, in which there is a near-perfect correlation between our level of confidence and our level of certainty of the future world around us.

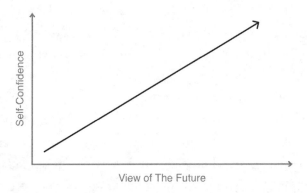

Figure 1.1 Our self-confidence and our outlook on the future are tightly correlated...

Source: Financial Insyghts

The reality, however, is that the future is in no way correlated to our level of confidence. The future is going to be what it is going to be whether we are confident about it or not. Although our preparation and attitude might improve our ability to cope with what the future holds, as much as we may want—and at times truly believe—otherwise, our level of confidence won't determine what is ahead. I try to capture this in Figure 1.2 with the horizontal line.

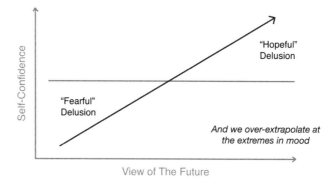

Figure 1.2 ...but the future is what it is and we over-extrapolate at the extremes in mood.
Source: Financial Insyghts

To me this is an important element of mood—particularly for investors—because, as Figure 1.2 suggests, it introduces the clear potential for us to over- and underestimate what is ahead due to changes in our level of confidence. I've come to think of this as our "hopeful delusion" when our mood rises and our "fearful delusion" when our mood falls. But as if that weren't bad enough, the more positive or negative our mood, the more we are naturally inclined (for better and for worse) to extrapolate those delusions into the future. Take one look at analyst earnings estimates and price targets at a major peak or trough of a stock and you'll see precisely what I mean. Few groups fall victim to the extrapolation effects of "hopeful delusion" and "fearful delusion" as repeatedly as the equity analyst community.

The more confident we are, the more into the future we think we can see and the more we extrapolate our current assessment of what we see as certain into future periods. And when our confidence and mood are extremely high, we naturally foresee great things ahead for some time to come.

The opposite, however, is true as our level of confidence deteriorates. In those times, we do the reverse and extrapolate more and more negative outcomes further and further out as our mood drops. Without even realizing why it is the case, we see things as becoming more and more hopeless. I have no doubt, for example, that at the very bottom of the Great Depression most Americans thought life would be uncertain forever—an extreme example of the extrapolation of fearful delusion.

As you'll see, these delusions play a critical role in our preferences and in our decision-making processes. They are a key underlying element to both asset bubbles and panics. They also bring into serious doubt whether we or any market are really ever truly rational at all!

The Two-Headed Coin of Certainty

Human behavior being what it is, when things go the way we were "certain" that they should have gone, we eagerly take the credit for the outcome—and in business, managers expect to be paid for the result arguing that they were skillful and that "Things went exactly according to plan." On the other hand, when things don't go the way we were "certain" they should have gone, we are quick to lay blame at the feet of market uncertainty—and most managers expect to be held immune from the result by arguing "Who could have known?"

In June 2011, Wells Fargo exited the reverse mortgage business and in its related press release stated that "The decision was made based on today's unpredictable home values."[1]

---

[1] Wells Fargo Corporation, "Wells Fargo Home Mortgage Discontinues Home Equity Conversion Mortgages," www.wellsfargo.com/press/2011/20110616_Mortgage (June 16, 2011).

What I love about this statement is that it suggests that when Wells Fargo entered the reverse mortgage business in 1990, the company thought that home values were predictable. (If unpredictable = exit, doesn't predictable = enter?)

The reality is that home values were no more or no less predictable in 2011 than they were in 1990. But Wells Fargo believed they were—as did many of us. To enter into a 15- or 20-year reverse mortgage, Well Fargo had to believe that home prices were predictable well into the future.

When we are confident we believe that everything is predictable (and in fact, "positively" predictable). When we are not confident, things are unpredictable. "Hopeful delusion" is replaced by "fearful delusion" as our mood deteriorates.

And it can happen quickly, too. In the summer of 2007, the most overused word in the financial services vernacular was "Goldilocks" because everything from the markets to the economy was "just right"—a perfect example of "hopeful delusion." Needless to say, not twelve months later, "fearful delusion" had set in with many expressing concern about the stability of the entire global financial system.

From my perspective, though, all of this begs the question as to whether investors overpay managers (both corporate and asset) in good times *and* in bad—rewarding most of them for luck (instead of skill) in good times while also accepting the excuse of unpredictability in bad.

Even worse, I'd argue that we over-reward managers for entering and exiting businesses at precisely the wrong times. From a return perspective, the best opportunities exist when markets perceive the greatest level of uncertainty, not the reverse.

As Wells Fargo's press release suggests, few companies that enter a business at the wrong time have the stomach to hold on until the peak of uncertainty passes. For those with patience, however, there is nothing like an endless stream of exiting suppliers—all blaming "unpredictable" values—to suggest that there is enormous opportunity ahead.

To me, the best questions that analysts, investors, and boards of directors can ask management relate to issues of certainty. What does management know for certain, and why? At least with regard to investments, the more certain people are (and the more people who share that certainty) the less certain that outcome is likely to be.

The Continuum of Social Mood

With all of that as background, Figure 1.3 presents what I see as the continuum of our own mood and confidence levels with our weakest mood level at the bottom left of the chart and our strongest level at the upper right.

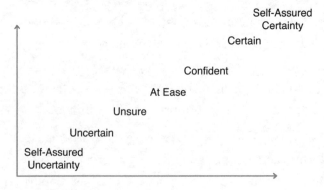

Figure 1.3 Continuum of social mood
Source: Financial Insyghts

I chose the term *self-assured certainty* for the peak expression of mood (and *self-assured uncertainty* for the trough) because as I looked at the behaviors and decision-making processes at both extremes, I felt it was important to pick up what I see as the consequential behavioral characteristics of the "delusional" elements I just discussed.

At the top, for example, not only are we certain, but we are certain of being certain. It is certainty squared. As I discuss in Chapter 3, we act like that, too. Likewise, at troughs in mood, it feels like uncertainty squared as well. At the very bottom, we are certain that nothing is certain. The entire foundation of our confidence is shaken.

Most investment advisors and brokers try to present these thoughts in "emotion curves" like the one shown in Figure 1.4 from my friend Jeff Saut of Raymond James.

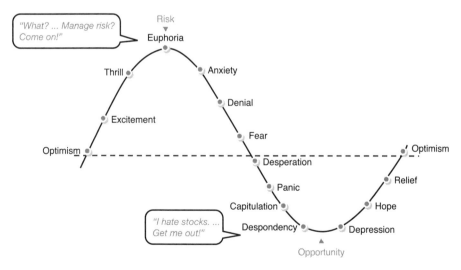

Figure 1.4 Investors' emotion curve

Source: Jeff Saut, Raymond James

To me, it is enormously helpful in moments of market turbulence, for example, to be able to step back and to distinguish self-assured uncertainty from panic or even despondency and conversely at major peaks to separate "self-assured certainty" from "euphoria;" to split mood and mood's related preferences and decision-making characteristics from the emotions we exhibit. By distinguishing between the cause and the effect, I think it is much easier to see euphoria (and the specific behaviors that naturally go along with it) as a real-time sign of peak self-assured certainty and a reason to sell, rather than an emotion into which one can be easily swept.

By better understanding mood, we can better see and respond to market opportunities rather than merely react alongside the rest of the crowd.

The Asymmetry of Rising and Falling Mood

Charts such as the "emotion curve" in Figure 1.4 suggest that the migration from peak to trough emotion follows a natural sine curve–like progression. The reality, however, is often far different.

When our children were young, we suggested that trust is like a Lego tower. It takes a long time to build it up brick by brick, but it can be destroyed quickly. The same is true with the confidence reflected in individual stocks and stock indices. A long, protracted rise in price is often followed by a quick, steep decline. Bull markets last longer than bear markets. Hopefully it is now easier to understand why that would be the case.

I highlight this point here because many investment strategies presume not only regular tide–like market movements up and down, but, more importantly, consistent liquidity and orderly market conditions at all points in the cycle in which to execute them as well.

Needless to say, steep declines in confidence are likely to be accompanied by commensurately steep drops in market prices and market liquidity as market participants curtail their risk-taking as their own levels of confidence fall.

But there is another aspect to the asymmetry of rising and falling mood that I think is also important: our seemingly insatiable desire for certainty itself.

Would you buy an investment from someone who is not confident about that investment's expected result? Would you take seriously the comments on Bloomberg or CNBC of a seemingly less-than-confident money manager?

I strongly doubt it. In the investment world, as in other businesses and in politics, we associate greater and greater levels of self-confidence in others with more certain outcomes. But consider for a moment that, in the world of investing, rising confidence and rising prices go together. Not surprisingly, as a result, we actually want and purchase more, not less, of a stock or commodity the higher the price rises (although most people don't realize this). As the greatest potential certainty for price appreciation is when the price of a stock is low, not high, investors routinely overpay for what they perceive to be a greater certainty.

I come back to this point throughout the book, but I think it is important to consider how dramatic the price consequences can be when investors in any asset realize that they have overpaid for what they thought was certain.

Perceived certainty is until it isn't. And as we abhor uncertainty, we then act accordingly, particularly with our money and investments.

Individual Versus Social Mood

If our own mood is the manifestation of our own level of self-confidence, then *social mood* can be thought of as the aggregate outcome of all of our individual moods put together. That is to say, social mood is our collective confidence.

I'd note, though, that even our own moods are rarely ever truly our own. At both an individual and collective level, our moods reflect our own interconnectivity with the world around us. Your personal mood, for example, incorporates the mood of your family, your work associates, members of your church, your book club, and so on. Your partner's mood picks up his or her network of family, friends, and professional and social affiliations. Together your collective mood, as a couple, folds in elements of them all.

I like to think of all of these social interconnection points as mood mirrors. Sometimes these mirrors reflect your herds' mood on you, and at other times these mirrors reflect your mood on them. Like it or not, though, your mood reflects the mood of the various herds you run with. You share their beliefs and they yours, and together, through an iterative and interactive process, your underlying mood is shaped and your brain then chooses a course of action that you believe is best.

That is how mood is formed for each of us, and how ultimately social mood comes together in aggregate. It is not just the sum of the parts, but the sum of the interactions (and re-interactions) of the parts that drive mood.

As noted in the Introduction, socionomists have deduced from the evidence that social mood is a natural product of human interaction and our natural herding instinct. As one who watches the interplay of social mood and the markets, I can say that nowhere does this iterative process become clearer than in the formations and re-formations of various "consensus trades"—where investors go from sharing one clear belief in what security or strategy will outperform another. Particularly for the retail investor, I think it is important to realize that in the investment world, they are often the very last to see and to participate in these collective iteratively formed "crowded trades" of the herd.

Measuring Mood

So, how does one best measure social mood?

For the U.S. as a whole, economists and many investors tend to look at one or more of the three major consumer mood indices: the Conference Board's Consumer Confidence Index®, the Thompson Reuters/University of Michigan Index of Consumer Sentiment®, and the Bloomberg Consumer Comfort Index®. Each has its own methodology and subcategories, but if you were to plot one on top of the other, you would see that they form very similar patterns over time. Unfortunately, as they all involve a survey process, they are often a lagging indicator. Of the three, I find the Bloomberg index most useful because it is published weekly, rather than monthly. Still, it too is lagged, as it reflects a four-week rolling average.

Bob Prechter offers that an even better measure of mood than the three major confidence indices, however, is the market itself. With a few minor caveats that I come back to in Chapter 8, "Social Mood and the Markets Today: So Where Are We?," I agree that the broad market indices (the S&P 500 and the Dow Jones Industrial Average) are the best real-time social mood barometer out there. They rise as our mood improves and fall as our mood deteriorates. Markets are moved by changes in our mood.

I realize for many this runs counter to the cause and effect concept suggested by others that rising markets lift our mood whereas falling markets result in a drop in our mood. As you'll see in Chapter 2, the ways in which changes in mood affect our preferences and our decision-making processes I believe make it clear that markets are moved by changes in our mood and not the other way around.

Acts of God and Other Exogenous Events

Having suggested that mood changes cause market movements, I'd like to pause to discuss acts of God and other exogenous events that appear to move the markets, in some cases dramatically.

Most investors (and certainly the financial press) lump together everything from hurricanes and tornados to corporate earnings and actions by the Federal Reserve as reasons for market movements up and down. At the risk of splitting hairs too finely, I'd encourage you to consider man-made exogenous events distinct from acts of God. As I hope becomes clear from this book, the decision-making processes behind man-made "events" reflect the same mood as the market itself.

Obviously, there is no human decision-making process behind a tornado, hurricane, earthquake, or other act of God. But there is a decision-making process in our own reaction to natural disasters, and mood plays a huge role in that process.

Looking at the stock market chart of the Dow Jones Industrial Average in 2005 that's shown in Figure 1.5, it would be very hard to point to Hurricane Katrina. (It occurred in late August.) Then again, on a chart of Japan's Nikkei index for 2011 (see Figure 1.6), it's all but impossible to miss the tsunami that occurred in March.

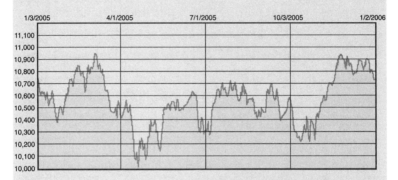

Figure 1.5 Hurricane Katrina and The Dow Jones Industrial Average in 2005

Source: Yahoo! (chart)/CSI (data). Reproduced with permission of Yahoo! Inc. © 2012 Yahoo! Inc. YAHOO! and the YAHOO! logo are registered trademarks of Yahoo! Inc.

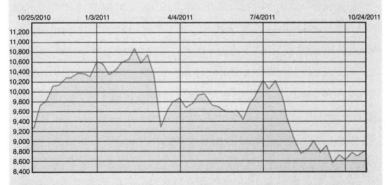

Figure 1.6 The Japanese Earthquake/Tsunami and the Nikkei 225 in 2011

Source: Yahoo! (chart)/CSI (data). Reproduced with permission of Yahoo! Inc. © 2012 Yahoo! Inc. YAHOO! and the YAHOO! logo are registered trademarks of Yahoo! Inc.

So why is that the case?

In periods of rising mood, as was the case in the U.S. during 2005, our rising confidence enabled us to see past the disaster and see the economic opportunities still ahead. In periods of falling mood, as was the case in Japan during 2011, we saw only the adverse consequences and the uncertainty created by the disaster.

As I noted earlier, markets react differently to near-identical news every day. One day markets rise on positive earnings reports and on another day they fall. The same is true with acts of God and other non-financial events. I have more examples later in the book, the market's reaction to which I expect will surprise you. As you'll see, what is logical to us is entirely situational—it depends precisely on the level and direction of our mood (rising or falling) at a given time.

Social Mood and the Media

I would like to pause here to discuss how social mood and the media interact. From my perspective, media (online, print, television, radio, Facebook, Twitter, and so on) are all just more social interconnection points that serve as mirrors reflecting both the herd's mood on you and your mood back on the herd.

Too many investors read the papers or watch television just for the news, instead of for the real-time indicator of social mood that they are. Remember, headlines are meant to sell papers and to draw you into online articles, so they are specifically written to resonate with your mood as a reader. As a result, all headlines and news stories act as mirrors on how you really feel, often without you even realizing it.

Let me give you an example of what I mean. On July 27, 2011, the following were some of the major headlines in the print edition of *The Wall Street Journal*:

"Boehner Plan Faces Rebellion"

"Banks Spar Over Loan Settlement"

"BP Results Frustrate Investors"

"Funds Could Fizzle"

"Home Sales, Prices Reflect Malaise"

"Beijing Blames 'Foreign Technology'"

"Wary Firms Opt For Temp Staff"

"Under Pressure, McDonald's Adds Apples to Kids Meals"

"Watchdog Sees Financial Weak Spots"

"At Soros, Family Is Foremost"

"Money Funds Dial Down Risk"

"UBS Is Forced to Scale Back"

"Deutsche Bank Draws Criticism on CEO Move"

So what were the underlying "reflecting" mood messages for each headline? How about these:

"Boehner Plan Faces Rebellion"	"Rebellion" = social unrest
"Banks Spar Over Loan Settlement"	"Spar" = adversarial relationships
"BP Results Frustrate Investors"	"Frustrate" = hindrance
"Funds Could Fizzle"	"Fizzle" = fear of what could happen in the future
"Home Sales, Prices Reflect Malaise"	"Malaise" = discontent
"Beijing Blames 'Foreign Technology'"	"Blames" = fault
"Wary Firms Opt For Temp Staff"	"Wary" = uneasiness
"Under Pressure, McDonald's Adds Apples to Kids Meals"	"Under Pressure" = unwillingness

"Watchdog Sees Financial Weak Spots"	"Weak" = unable
"At Soros, Family Is Foremost"	"Family Is Foremost" = self-interest
"Money Funds Dial Down Risk"	"Dial Down Risk" = fear
"UBS Is Forced to Scale Back"	"Scale Back" = retrenchment
"Deutsche Bank Draws Criticism on CEO Move"	"Criticism" = disapproval

From my perspective, these headlines did a great job of capturing our mood at the time; however, I saw none of this yet captured in market prices. During the next week, however, stocks fell precipitously. Even more, I'd note that people rioted in London and set fire to cars in Germany and Ireland, and, not surprisingly, reported consumer confidence plummeted in August.

When I saw the headlines, I felt like our mood had deteriorated significantly, but the market's actions did not yet reflect that.

Note that the reverse can also be true, however. Headlines and the media can often be late in capturing our mood. For example, I love all of those "market plummeting" news specials on CNBC and Bloomberg. They are great indicators of a pending change in market direction. Why? Because they pull together both emotion (with all the scary music that naturally accompanies those programs) and our collective sense of uncertainty. And if it is on national television, we must *all* be feeling it, too.

The same is true for many magazine covers. They are often much better contrarian indicators than anything. For example, *The Economist* featured a particularly grim cover on its October 1, 2011 issue with the headline, "Until politicians actually do something about the world economy... BE AFRAID," with "BE AFRAID" in big bold red lettering in the center no less. That cover coincided perfectly with a major market bottom, following which the S&P bounced more than 20% in less than a month!

More often than not, investors fall victim to the mood and emotion reflected in the media and do precisely the wrong thing in response. Rather than readily accepting headlines and cover stories as fact, investors would be much wiser to ask themselves whether the "certainty" reflected on magazine covers and news stories all around them is already reflected in market prices. When it is, a significant market turn may be at hand.

Mood Groups

One of the important aspects of how social mood comes together is that it enables moods to be local, regional, national, or even global in nature. Europe's social mood is different from Asia's, and Germany's is distinct from Greece's. Mood can also be industry and company specific. No doubt the mood inside of HP today is very different from the mood at Dell or Apple, for example.

I believe that it is the consistency in mood, however, that drives correlations within and across markets. I return to this topic in Chapter 8, when I look at the potential role communications technology may play in our current market mood overall.

Final Thoughts

I realize for many readers the notion that the markets are driven by changes in our confidence level, rather than external, exogenous events, might be difficult to believe—particularly as it turns most financial news media cause and effect on its head. I also appreciate that for some the idea that what we think is logical is somehow tied to mood and, therefore, subject to constant change may also be disturbing. And I am sure, too, that there are more than a few economists who might be bothered by the notion that we and the markets are rarely, if ever, rational. But the consistent, repeating patterns of near-identical, concurrent behaviors across social movements, politics, and financial markets—even the arts—over long periods of history suggests that there is something else, beyond events, that underlies our actions.

As Mark Twain put it, history may not repeat, but it certainly rhymes.

I believe it all ties to confidence, and in Chapter 2, I tackle how and why that is the case.

2

Horizon Preference: How Mood Affects Our Decision Making

Although I found the principles of socionomics and the causal relationship between mood and events of great interest, I struggled for a long time with specifically how and why mood could alter outcomes. This led me to look very closely at how mood affects our decision-making processes and, more specifically, what we see as logical choices (our preferences) based on our various levels of confidence. In this chapter, I discuss these topics.

To see how mood directly affects our decision-making processes, I am going to borrow from one of the best artificial mood creators I know of: the rollercoaster. Nothing does a better job of creating what I call self-assured uncertainty (where we are certain of being uncertain) in a hurry than the click, click, click of the coaster as it slowly begins its ascent skyward at the beginning of the ride. And I love how most coasters pause at the very, very top of the hill as if to put an exclamation point on the uncertain experience we are about to face, giving us a final second or two to think about what is immediately ahead.

But consider for a moment what it is that we really do think about in that instant just before the brake is released and the cars plummet down the track.

- **Who** are we thinking about?
- **Where** are we thinking about?
- **When** are we thinking about?

I realize these may seem like unusual questions, but I believe that at moments of peak self-assured uncertainty, such as we experience at the top of a rollercoaster, no one is thinking about a long lost cousin, issues in another part of the amusement park (let alone elsewhere in the world), or even about a pressing homework assignment or supposedly urgent work project due next week.

No—when certainty is most in doubt and confidence most shaken, the answers to the three questions are clear and unambiguous.

And those answers are

- **Me**
- **Here**
- **Now**

In fact, I would swear that right before the cars plummet down the track, those white-knuckled silent prayers are almost audible: "Just get me through the next 26 seconds on this rollercoaster, and I promise I'll..."

- **Me**
- **Here**
- **Now**

The Horizon Preference Continuum

At moments of peak uncertainty our world is intensely small (see Figure 2.1). It's me—not you or anyone else. It's here—not across the park, across the city, or across the world. And it's now—not tomorrow, next week, or next year.

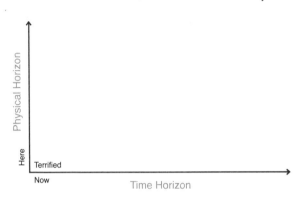

Figure 2.1 In extreme fear, our world is very small.
Source: Financial Insyghts

I believe that the reason we respond this way is physiological. It is how our bodies and minds cope with the stress arising from uncertainty. In times of uncertainty, we shut out unnecessary complexity and anything that is extraneous to survival. (And at our greatest levels of stress or shock, the body even goes so far as to shut down unnecessary functions inside our bodies, too.) It is simply how we are wired.

To return to the rollercoaster analogy I offered earlier, consider for a second what happens the moment after the ride ends. Suddenly we are eagerly talking to the person next to us and discussing what ride we might take next. "Me" is now "us"—we begin to herd. And "here" and "now" have expanded to incorporate somewhere across the amusement park and later in the day.

To analogize, it is as if our minds have been fitted with variable lens goggles that automatically manage our peripheral vision in three dimensions: a physical horizon, a time horizon, and a relationship horizon, where our vision in all three dimensions is based on our level of confidence. I've come to think of this 3-D peripheral vision as our *Horizon Preference*. It is what we naturally, and often unknowingly, prefer based on our level of mood.

Where we are and how we see and deal with the world around us is based on our mood along a continuum from "me, here, now" to "us, everywhere, forever."

I believe that in times of rising mood our Horizon Preference naturally expands without us even realizing it; conversely, when our mood falls, our Horizon Preference contracts. As our confidence grows, so too does the world in which we want to participate. As our confidence falls, we naturally want to pull back and retreat from that world as well. Again, this is a part of our herding instinct and how we are coded for survival.

Our lives, individually and collectively, are spent moving up and down a continuum of confidence with corresponding shifts in our Horizon Preference. And we can measure it looking at both time and geographic horizons (see Figure 2.2).

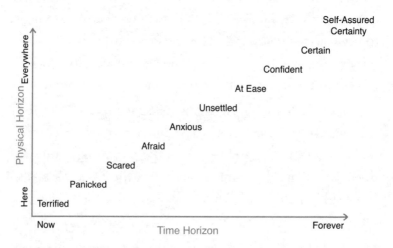

Figure 2.2 Our outlook on time and space reflects our mood...
Source: Financial Insyghts

And relationships, too (see Figure 2.3).

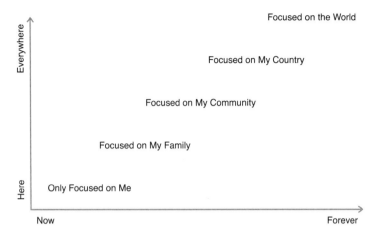

Figure 2.3 ...Changes in our mood also affect our relationships
Source: Financial Insyghts

Our location and direction on the Horizon Preference continuum directly affects our judgment. It determines why it can make sense to us to want to join a group on one day, and why it can be just as logical to us that we would want to exit that same organization on another. Why we would want to buy homes eagerly at higher and higher prices one year, and then a mere two years later be desperate to rent even with record low interest rates and housing affordability. In one case we are making decisions during rising mood and in the other we are making decisions during declining mood.

This is how I believe mood translates to the events that we witness every day—socially, politically, and economically. Mood determines our Horizon Preference, which in turn—without us even realizing it—drives what we see as logical and the decisions we make.

Put simply, our actions are ruled by our level of confidence, both individually and as a collective whole.

Beginning to Use Horizon Preference

In a moment, I talk specifically about the decision-making processes that accompany both rising and falling moods. Before doing that, though, I encourage you to consider the world today and the headlines and events that you see around you. Looking at the charts in Figures 2.2 and 2.3, does what you see around you in business, politics, and the economy suggest an upward-right or a lower-left migration in mood—"me, here, now" or "us, everywhere, forever"? If you think mood peaked and we are in a period of deteriorating mood, when do you think the peak was and why? On the other hand, if you see mood rising, what specific evidence of "us, everywhere, forever" would you expect to see at the very top?

Think about the headlines I presented in Chapter 1, "Understanding Social Mood"; all of them suggested to me a significant "lower-left" move in late July 2011. Even billionaire George Soros—by closing his fund to all but his family (a less "us" and more "me" decision)—was moving toward the lower left (and probably not even realizing it)! But note that in late July the lower-left move in Horizon Preference reflected in the headlines had not yet been priced into stock market values.

To me the greatest opportunities that exist for investors, across multiple time frames, is when our mood has not yet been reflected in market prices.

Logical Decision Making in Periods of Rising Social Mood

In looking at Horizon Preference in its three dimensions, with rising confidence (and a move to the upper right) our decisions consistently reflect

- Longer and longer time horizons and greater permanence (time)

- Greater and greater efforts at physical expansion, exploration, and greater globalism (physical)

- More and more inclusiveness, rising trust in others, generosity, and comfort with increasing organizational complexity, innovation, and size (relational)

While not meant to be exhaustive by any means, let me provide some examples of the kinds of decisions that I believe naturally accompany rising mood thanks to expanding Horizon Preference:

For corporations:

- Acquisitions—investments in property, plant, and equipment

- Permanent hiring

- Deployment of "just in time" inventory management systems

- Foreign market expansion (both distribution and sourcing)

- Business partnerships and joint ventures

- Diversity initiatives

- Scorecard and stock-based compensation plans

- Deployment of innovative technologies
- Greater use of debt and financial leverage/stock buybacks[1]
- Membership in trade groups and associations

For financial institutions:

- More aggressive loan pricing
- Looser underwriting standards
- Lower absolute capital levels and the increased use of innovative hybrid capital
- Greater reliance on short-term funding
- Increases in mark-to-market securities holdings
- Greater emphasis on cross-selling initiatives
- Greater societal willingness toward deregulation
- Increasing standardization of regulations, particularly across borders
- Advertising of "global" capabilities

For individuals:

- More credit purchases
- Greater stock ownership
- Broader homeownership with larger and larger homes
- Greater enrollment in four-year colleges
- Growing community involvement
- Greater philanthropy

---

[1] John Nofsinger, 2005. "Social Mood and Financial Economics." *Journal of Behavioral Finance* 6:3, 144-160.

For political institutions:

- Greater compromise and recognition of collective success
- Re-elections and growing incumbency
- Mounting bipartisanship
- Increases in cross-border treaties
- Fewer duties, tariffs, and barriers to immigration
- Reductions in foreign-exchange controls

I hope after looking at these lists it is easy to see how the expansion of the three dimensions of time, space, and relationships captured in Horizon Preference are evident in our decisions during periods of rising mood. Even more, I hope the lists help you to appreciate what an enormous flywheel rising confidence is to an economy, as it drives decisions across the public and private sectors that are both uniformly positive and symbiotic.

One of the ways that I believe that rising confidence most affects growth is in the way changes in time preference affect our economic decisions. In periods of weak social mood, most economic decisions are based strictly on current income levels. (And in periods of very severe downturns in mood, even current income is viewed as entirely temporary.)

As mood improves, however, the uncertainties associated with current income are replaced by certainties that go along with more permanent wealth. Although economists refer to this as the *wealth effect* I think that it is more the *rising mood effect*; rising mood expands our Horizon Preference (see Figure 2.4).

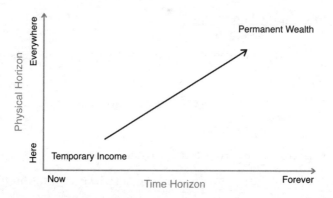

Figure 2.4 The real wealth effect?

Source: Financial Insyghts

Why I think this is so important is because it is not just consumer consumption patterns that are affected by the so-called wealth effect. Borrowing and lending behaviors also change (with consumers more eager to take on credit and banks more eager to extend it as mood improves) and investment activities at both an individual and a corporate level reflect greater and greater forecasted certainty.

I come back to this point later when I discuss where I think we are today in Chapter 8, "Social Mood and the Markets Today: So Where Are We?," but consider the enormous number of decisions over the past 30 years that were made across the public and private sectors predicated on the self-assured certainty of future wealth. From residential housing to aircraft to retail consumer goods, there were significant investments based on the extrapolation of extremely positive trends well into the future.

Rising mood also provides a natural tailwind for investors as it brings with it an enormous earnings multiplier effect as sales rise, costs fall, markets expand, and so on. Nowhere is that captured better than in forward-looking price-earnings (P/E) ratios. Thanks to improving Horizon Preference our visibility expands—measured in both time and space (suggesting bigger and longer growth opportunities ahead)—and at the same time (thanks to rising societal trust) we lower the discount rate we use to present future value opportunities.

As the chart from J.P. Morgan in Figure 2.5 suggests, the correlation between consumer sentiment and forward P/E ratios is statistically significant.

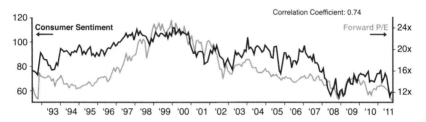

Figure 2.5 Mood and forward P/E ratios correlate
Source: J.P. Morgan

To me, this makes very natural sense. As I noted earlier, both confidence and stock prices are forward looking.

The 1950s and Early 1960s

Because, as Mark Twain shared, history "rhymes," I think it may be helpful to reflect on a period of time in which the decisions that naturally accompany rising confidence and expanding Horizon Preference offered earlier were clear. To me, one great example is the late 1950s and early 1960s during the rollout of national television and the expansion of jet air travel both in the U.S. and internationally. This period also saw the election of the first Irish-Catholic president (John F. Kennedy), the space race, and Kennedy's challenge to put a man on the moon. Dr. Martin Luther King, Jr. delivered his "I have a dream" speech and the Civil

Rights Movement made great strides. The Mustang was launched and multinational conglomerates, such as International Telephone and Telegraph (ITT), flourished. ITT itself, for example, acquired more than 300 companies in the 1960s, including Sheraton Hotels, Wonder Bread, The Hartford, and even Avis Rent-a-Car. It was an "us, everywhere, forever" confidence level applied to "everything." But consider too that investors shared this same strong confidence level, handsomely rewarding the growing complexity of multinational conglomerates at every turn.

This is not to say that bad things didn't happen during this same period. There were wars, coups, and plenty of other negative events. But note that even on the day Kennedy was shot, the stock market dropped by just 2.9%—hardly horrendous when compared to what we have seen over the past several years—and stocks actually rose 4.5% on the next trading day. That's one of the best single-day returns of the entire twentieth century, and the market continued to go higher, gaining 25% over the next 12 months![2]

Yes, in the aftermath of the assassination, the world was very sad—a strong natural, emotional reaction to the tragic event—but rising mood drove the decision making. To me, this is a perfect example of the behavioral distinction between mood/confidence and emotion.

Finally, consider what the recent selection of early 1960s-era shows such as *Mad Men*, *Pan Am*, and even *The Playboy Club* says about us and our own mood today. To me, there is no coincidence to the current romanticizing of these supposed "good old days."

[2] Jason Zweig, "What we can learn from history," *Money*, p. S4, Fall 2001.

Logical Decision Making in Periods of Falling Social Mood

Whereas rising mood and improving Horizon Preference act like a positive flywheel, declining mood and deteriorating Horizon Preference serve more as a fly in the ointment.

Specifically, during periods of falling mood our decisions reflect the following:

- Shorter and shorter time horizons and a mounting sense that things are temporary (time)
- Greater physical contraction and rising nationalism/localism (physical)
- Rising exclusionism, scrutiny, selfishness, and discomfort with complexity, size, and innovation (relational)

So how do these aspects manifest themselves?

For corporations:

- Divestitures, plant closings, and consolidations
- Job reductions and temporary hiring rather than permanent hiring
- Deployment of "just in case" inventory management systems
- Market and product line retrenchment
- Adversarial relationships between partners, suppliers, customers, and so on
- Litigation
- Streamlining, simplification, and emphasis on traditional technologies
- Emphasis on risk management
- Greater use of equity and on-balance sheet hoarding of cash

For financial institutions:

- Stricter loan underwriting standards
- Risk aversion
- Higher absolute and better quality capital
- Emphasis on liquidity
- Reduction in mark-to-market securities
- Regulatory scrutiny and regulated pricing
- Advertising "local" decision making

For individuals:

- Cash and debit purchases
- Bond investing
- Home rental
- Public higher education
- Civil unrest

For political institutions:

- Leaders and other elected officials voted out of office
- Extremism
- Partisanship
- Increasing nationalism

The Late 1960s and Early 1970s

If the late 1950s and early 1960s reflected rising social mood, the late 1960s and early 1970s mirrored the reverse. Watergate, Wounded Knee, Kent State, the Pentagon Papers, and the Chicago Seven filled the headlines. ITT became embroiled in a Congressional investigation into activities of the CIA in Chile. And the Apollo program ceased just three years after successfully landing a man on the moon. College attendance fell. Plane hijackings surged, and in August 1972 TWA and American Airlines began inspecting luggage on planes. The United States military came home from Vietnam without a clear victory and Exxon was criticized by Congress for profiting from the oil embargo with Senator Henry Jackson describing Exxon's actions as a "flagrant case of corporate disloyalty to the United States government."[3]

Again, consider what it says about our mood today that during the past two years Hollywood offered updated versions of both *True Grit* (1969) and *Planet of the Apes* (1968). And just as in 1968's *Night of the Living Dead*, zombies seem to be everywhere today. How about *That '70s Show*? While admittedly the show covers 1976–1979, to me it is very interesting that rather than romanticizing the period, we now choose to laugh at its awkwardness. Finally, note the tremendous success of the PBS Masterpiece Theatre series *Downton Abbey* and its similarities to the 1971–1975 series *Upstairs, Downstairs*. Talk about a series that more than "rhymes" and that picks up the growing economic divide/99% versus 1% theme of Occupy Wall Street.

---

[3] Daniel, Clifton, ed. *Chronicle of the 20th Century* (Mount Kisco, NY: Chronicle Publications, 1987), 1074.

For business managers and investors (not to mention policymakers) I think it is important to recognize that social mood is a collective experience both good and bad. What is happening in manufacturing facilities, in political chambers, on the stage on Broadway, or in movie theaters and on the streets are all likely to be concurrent manifestations of the same underlying mood that is reflected in stocks.

To go back to early August 2011, for example, the sudden drop in stock prices, the clear partisanship in Washington, the precipitous decline in U.S. consumer gas consumption (to a 10-year low) and the riots in London were not a coincidence; they were concurrent reflections of the same significant lower-left migration in Horizon Preference (see Figure 2.6). It was "me, here, and now" in 3-D: politically, socially, and economically. Not surprisingly, then, it marked the low for the FTSE 100 for the entire year.

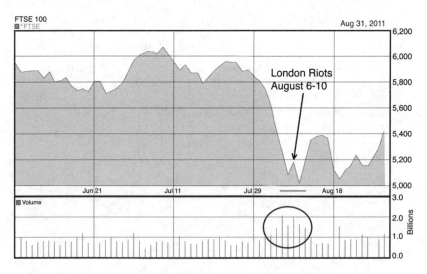

Figure 2.6 The London riots coincided with the August 2011 low in the FTSE 100

Source: Yahoo! (chart)/ CSI (data). Reproduced with permission of Yahoo! Inc. © 2012 Yahoo! Inc. YAHOO! and the YAHOO! logo are registered trademarks of Yahoo! Inc.

Banks and Declines in Social Mood

From my perspective there are few industries more adversely affected by downturns in social mood than banking. For banks, declining confidence generates a toxic combination of asset value deflation and liability inflation at precisely the same time when, due to lower confidence levels, everyone from the markets to regulators to depositors wants these firms to hold more capital.

Nowhere has this been clearer over the past three years than at a firm like Bank of America. On the asset side, declining confidence has resulted in lower credit demand and rising delinquencies coupled with more stringent credit standards and general risk aversion; meanwhile mark-to-market securities holdings (stocks and bonds that a firm would typically buy because it anticipated a near-term rise in their value) have been written down and cross-selling has declined. Finally, both regulatory and public sentiment have constrained the bank's ability to raise prices, with the Bank's proposed $5.00-per-month debit card fee receiving particularly fierce condemnation from both consumers and public officials.

On the liability side of the balance sheet, during the banking crisis, BofA's borrowing costs increased as many depositors and most non-deposit creditors sought greater yields while the Bank concurrently tried to lengthen its debt maturities to reduce liquidity risk. Then, of course, there has been massive litigation, adding even more liabilities to the balance sheet.

Finally, within capital, BofA has faced any number of challenges as the regulators and the markets have repeatedly sought both more and better quality equity, forcing the firm in response to sell off profitable businesses and other investments to close the gap.

For investors, I think it is important to recognize that because of their financial leverage (10 to 12:1 debt-to-equity ratios even in good times) and their susceptibility to asset deflation and liability inflation, banks are incredibly vulnerable to declining social mood. As a result, they are always one of the first industries to reflect social mood drops. Even more, the magnitude of their challenges are a great early indicator of what is to come for the rest of the economy.

(That said, I would also note that the reverse is true. When mood turns at the bottom, the intense valuation compression applied on the way down is often "released" with enormous price gains. For example from late-December 2011 to mid-March 2012, not even three full months, BofA stock more than doubled as mood improved and concerns about the Bank's financial condition abated.)[4]

Opportunities During Declining Social Mood

Many investors assume that everything goes down when mood drops and the market averages decline, but that is not necessarily the case. During 2010 and 2011, it was interesting to see how well companies like Facebook and Netflix

[4] Peter Atwater, "Banking on a Recovery: Understanding the Mood-Driven Decompression Trade" www.minyanville.com/sectors/financial/articles/compression-trade-decompression-trade-peter-atwater/3/22/2012/id/40026#ixzz1tckM458w. March 22, 2012.

did in the markets. To me these were the embodiment of a "me, here, now" declining social mood investment strategy (see Figure 2.7). And even Groupon—with its focus on local coupon offerings—fit the Horizon Preference migration to the lower left. So did the boom in multi-family housing as Americans opted to rent notwithstanding record housing affordability and record-low interest rates. Finally, and not surprisingly, gun makers like Sturm Ruger and pawnbrokers like First Cash Financial were on top-performing stock lists as well.

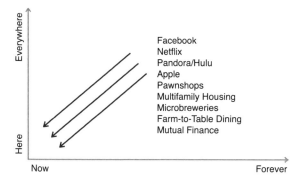

Figure 2.7 "Logical" 2011 business opportunities in a "me, here, now" economy
Source: Financial Insyghts

It was not just investors who responded to the "pure play" "me, here, now" opportunities arising from deteriorating social mood. Last August, during the same week protesters were rioting in London, *The Wall Street Journal* noted that Walmart, "which scours the globe seeking the lowest-cost suppliers,"[5] had begun to sell more locally grown fruits and vegetables, joining the locavore movement in an effort to satisfy changing consumer preferences.

---

[5] Miguel Bustillo and David Kesmodel, "'Local' Grows on Wal-Mart," *The Wall Street Journal*, August 1, 2011.

Finally, what about the "i" prefix for Apple's most successful products? Although it was initially intended to capture the "i" in Internet, I can't help but wonder whether today, in light of our declining mood, we've all come to better think of the "i" as capturing "I" as in *my* Mac, *my* phone, and *my* tablet/tv/movie screen. Better than any other company, I believe that Apple's entire product line aligned with consumers' natural desire for "me, here, now" technology solutions during a period of poor social mood.

Final Thoughts

Although many may suggest that it is pure coincidence, the recurring alignment of financial, social, political, and even cultural decisions that reflect a consistent time, physical, and relationship horizon suggests to me that our underlying mood matters. History rhymes, and multi-dimensionally at that.

Rising confidence broadens our Horizon Preference whereas falling confidence does the reverse. The good news for investors is that because the direction of our mood manifests itself in so many ways, there are abundant signs along the way to provide clues as to both where we are and where we are headed. If you know what to look for—and hopefully the lists offered earlier in the chapter will help you in the future—it is almost hard not to see examples every day.

I find that by focusing on objective measures of social mood—and the specific behaviors that I see that reflect either rising or falling levels of confidence—I can stay clear of the emotions of the market.

This begs the following question: If we move up and down along a continuum of rising and falling moods, how do we know when rising mood has peaked and falling mood has bottomed? How, using social mood, do we minimize our investment risks when we buy and sell?

To begin to answer those questions, I look at mood peaks next.

3

Market Peaks and All the Red Flags They Wave

After writing *Good to Great*, author Jim Collins wrote another book, *How the Mighty Fall*, in which he looked at the trajectory of corporate decline. In that book, he offers:

> *We anticipated that most companies fall from greatness because they become complacent—they fail to stimulate innovation, they fail to initiate bold action, they fail to ignite change, they just become lazy—and watch the world pass them by. It's a plausible theory, with a problem: it doesn't square with our data. Certainly, any enterprise that becomes complacent and refuses to change or innovate will eventually fall. But, and this is the surprising point, the companies in our analysis showed little evidence of complacency when they fell. Overreaching much better explains how the once-invincible self-destruct.*[1]

Of course it does. With self-assured certainty, coupled with the extreme extrapolation of today's success that naturally comes with peak hopeful delusion, how could companies not overreach at the top?! They perceive opportunity in almost every direction as far out as the eye can see. It is "us, everywhere, forever."

---

[1] Jim Collins, *How the Mighty Fall* (New York: HarperCollins, 2009), 46-47.

The Concept Stock Bubble

Although the past 20 years have given us many "peak mood experiences" and the corresponding bubbles to go along with them, I think few compare to the self-assured certainty that went along with the boom in concept stocks at the very peak of the dot-com bubble. (For those not familiar with the term "concept stocks," these were start-up, Internet-based companies that had little to no revenue; they were just "great ideas"—companies such as Pets.com and Webvan, which intended to sell pet accessories and groceries, respectively, online.)

What I love about the concept stock bubble (Figure 3.1) is not only the sheer ridiculousness of many of the companies themselves, but also what those companies said about the self-assured certainty of investors at that time. At the very top, investors were so confident of the transformational nature of the Internet that they believed that just about every Internet-based idea would be wildly successful well into the future. Heck, Webvan even convinced George Shaheen, then the CEO of Andersen Consulting (now Accenture) to quit his job to become that start-up's CEO!

Looking at many of the companies that went public near the peak of the dot.com bubble, you'd have thought that nothing could fail. So, of course there was absolutely no reason to be worried about the lack of current revenue. It was beyond a "Field of Dreams" mindset, it was, "If you build it, they and the rest of the world (if not the entire solar system) will come and they will all stay and we'll prosper forever!"

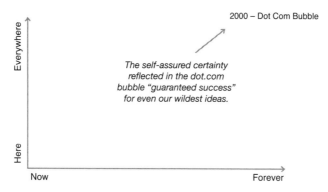

Figure 3.1 Why "concept stocks" were logical in 2000
Source: Financial Insyghts

In fact, when I talked about the concept stock bubble recently with one friend, she offered that at the very, very top, she was approached about an investment opportunity in a company that didn't even have an idea. Rather than building out an existing strategy, the company she was shown was going to use the money to first hire "the right people" who would then come up with the ideas!

Now that's self-assured certainty!

We do it over and over and over. For example, in 2008, in doing some research on market panics, I came across the following quote from Edward M. Shepard's 1888 book *The Life of Martin Van Buren:*

> *If the Erie Canal, finished in 1825, had rendered vast natural resources available, and had made its chief builder famous, why not like schemes prosper further west? The success of railroads was already established; and there was indefinite promise in the extensions of them already planned. In 1830 twenty-three miles had been constructed; in 1831 ninety-four miles; and in 1836 the total construction had risen to 1,273 miles.*[2]

[2] Edward M. Shepard, *Life of Martin Van Buren* (Boston: Houghton, Mifflin Company, 1888).

"Indefinite promise," extreme extrapolation, and more rhyming history. Railroads, canals, the Internet...we do it over and over and over. We overreach.

Big Truths

So if we repeatedly exhibit the same decision-making behavior at the very top, why don't we see it and stop ourselves from repeating the past? I think there are several reasons.

First, underlying every bubble is what I call a Big Truth: a statement that is both compelling and at the same time, if false, would draw the entire investment premise into doubt. It's something like "the Internet will change the world forever," "China will dominate the global economy," or "Western governments are the safest out there and they will never default on their sovereign debt."

The Big Truth is a very black-or-white statement. It either is or it isn't. Even more so, you can (or think you can) begin it with the words "obviously" or "of course." It is highly believable by people of all levels of sophistication. It is something everyone can easily understand.

But appreciate, too, that by the very top there has been plenty of data and experience to support that not only is the Big Truth true, it has been all but proved certain. There is a track record of success, and in the context of business I think it is important to appreciate that this success has been shared by everyone in the food chain—employees, customers, suppliers, analysts, investors, government officials, regulators, and so on. Everybody is in—even the skeptics.

At the very top it truly is "us"—all of us—and to me, one of the most important elements of a peak in mood is the saturation in our thinking that not only is the Big Truth certain, but what is great today will be only greater in the future (the "forever" quality). And there are often "everywhere" aspects, too. There is certainty that the opportunities are boundless, whether by geography, product line, or some other measure.

So why do even the skeptics climb aboard? I believe this again goes back to our herding instinct and our internal coding for survival. It is very hard (and very lonely—believe me I know from personal experience) to be a skeptic in a world in which everyone else exhibits self-assured certainty about what is ahead, especially as you watch them make a lot of money at it—which they are all too happy to remind you of.

It is for this reason that I believe one of the best indicators of a peak in mood—whether in an individual stock or commodity, or for the market as a whole—is its resemblance to middle school. Tops are awash in strident, hubris-filled, self-assured certainty, and doubters are not only outcasts; they are publicly vilified idiots. It's the seventh grade over and over again—an unfiltered, very black or very white world in which people either are or want to be in the "in crowd."

At the peak, those suggesting that prices are going to go down are not just nonbelievers, they are social outcasts drowned out by the crowd.

Abdication of Risk Management

If there is a second common behavioral element to peaks, it is in the area of risk management. At the very top, many corporate leaders openly ridicule their internal risk managers as obstacles to doing business; and many CEOs even go so far as to publicly overrule their risk teams, canceling hedges and entering into bold, long-term contracts that assume continued robust growth/price appreciation (an almost universal trait in commodity and energy sector peaks).

But what is so interesting to me about peak behavior is that with self-assured certainty, the rules of prudent risk management are not so much skirted as eliminated; the Big Truth makes them seemingly unnecessary. Rather than possibly considering that the consistent outcomes that have accompanied the Big Truth over an extended period of time as an exception (particularly to the natural cycles that accompany most business), corporate managers and investors begin to believe that this time truly is different, with all parties eagerly extrapolating the latest record results further and further into the future. At the peak, they mistake luck for skill.

If it's been nothing but up so far, of course the trend line will continue higher, if not accelerate! And remarkably (or maybe not so remarkably), most boards of directors eagerly concur. Rather than playing the role of prudent skeptic at the top, most boards look and act like a cheerleading squad for management, and even more so when they have been compensated in rapidly appreciating common stock and stock options.

And boards of directors are hardly alone in their confidence. I think it is also important to recognize that, thanks to peaking mood, the behavior of regulators, creditors, the ratings agencies, and other supposedly risk-focused organizations are not much different. At the very top, there is a collective abdication of risk management.

> **MF Global**
>
> I wrote these comments on risk management well before MF Global failed, and although it may take years for the precise sequence of events to be fully revealed, I strongly suspect that the existence of a Big Truth—in this case that CEO John Corzine is a great business leader and risk taker—and the abdication of risk management played an enormous role in the precipitous decline of the firm.

Organizational Complexity

A third consistent element of peaks is oversized organizational complexity. Whether it is through excessively large acquisitions, broad geographic expansion, or the addition of non-strategic businesses (where management and the board has no expertise), at the top, companies consistently display a Manifest Destiny–like need to be bigger and more far-reaching than ever. (And yes, journalist John O'Sullivan's introduction of the term Manifest Destiny in 1845 coincides very nicely with the ending of a bull market that started at the end of the War of 1812.) And so that it is said, mergers of equals, with their "I'm so confident that we can even be co-CEOs—literally 'us, everywhere, forever'" sentiment, are almost universally some of the most ill-timed reflections of peak mood ever!

ITT was a great example of oversized complexity in the 1960s with its far-flung businesses ranging from switchboards to rental cars, as was Tyco during the 1990s (complete with its own more-globalist Manifest Destiny name change from Tyco Laboratories, Inc. to Tyco International Ltd. [complete with an off-shore corporate headquarters move] near its peak). But these two companies are hardly alone. Having spent my entire career in banking, I witnessed firsthand an enormous complexity transformation as domestic commercial banks morphed into global financial services firms, and where, at the very top, the industry believed it could successfully deliver every product to every client everywhere in the world.

As mood peaks, companies believe there is boundless opportunity in every direction, and they eagerly add complexity in the belief they can harvest it all.

Novice and Naïve Entrants

A fourth trait of peaks is novice entrants. As discussed earlier, peak moods are filled with hubris that sucks everyone in at the very top. Peaks are a social vortex. But what I think few truly appreciate is that those who join last are most often the most naïve. They join not because they understand the underlying risks of the business (which at the top would be perceived by others to be nonexistent anyway) but because they see nothing but opportunity and because everyone else joined. They trust too much in both the Big Truth and the wisdom of the crowd. Rather than looking out the windshield, they use their rearview mirror to see what they think is ahead. They buy based on a "proven" track record and the confidence exhibited by others around them.

To me a perfect example of this phenomenon was the peak of the U.S. housing bubble in which there was a tsunami of novice entrants in every category from builders to appraisers, borrowers, originators, lenders, and so on. At the very top, the entire food chain was chock full of people with little to no experience. The same thing occurred at the top of the dot-com bubble, as house painters and cab drivers quit their day jobs to become day traders.

I saw plenty of examples of novice entrants at the top in banking, too. From Swiss-based banking giant UBS's ill-timed purchase of U.S.-based brokerage firm Paine Webber in 2000 to HSBC's acquisition of Household, the urge to merge at the top became insatiable. At the top, it was as if a front page, above the crease, *The Wall Street Journal* deal had become a required CEO merit badge, and the further afield from the firm's historic core business the acquisition was the better.

From my perspective, one of the best things an investor can do is to constantly assess the participants in the food chain—from management to suppliers to investors—and to objectively consider their experience and, more specifically, their appreciation for a business's underlying risks. New, naïve, and hope-filled participants, particularly after a significant rise in price, should be a yellow warning flag and a reason to seriously challenge the assumptions underpinning the Big Truth, particularly because naïveté coupled with the risk management abdication that accompanies peak mood quickly creates the opportunity to drive a business completely off the road far faster—and more severely—than most investors ever believe possible.

Credit, Architecture, and Other Signs of the Top

Finally, a fifth common element is the excessive use of leverage and credit. At its core, credit utilization (versus equity) reflects confidence by both borrower and lender alike.

And the more extreme it is (as reflected by rising leverage, the use of debt, particularly short-term debt, to fund activities such as stock repurchases and dividends) the more it likely reflects yet another sign of a broad systemic abdication of risk management.

There are plenty of other signs as well. Having been involved in the financial services industry for most of my career, nothing says "top" to me like a new bank headquarters building. The more opulent, insular, and impractical the better!

Citibank, for example, started planning the Citigroup Center—with its four legged-base and angled roof (see Figure 3.2)—in the early 1970s just as the markets were peaking.

Today, the skyline of Dallas is filled with built-at-the-top "memorials" to banks-gone-bust such as Interfirst, MCorp, Texas Commerce, and Allied Bank. All were built at the top.

Needless to say, Apple's new campus design has me scratching my head, as do London's new record-height "Shard" and Prince Alwaleed's record-breaking skyscraper that is to be built as part of a $20 billion new development in Saudi Arabia that will overlook the Red Sea. Like the Empire State Building, the World Trade Center, and the Burj before them, all of these buildings suggest caution.

I am not alone with these feelings. When Apple's new headquarters design was leaked to the public, *The New Yorker*'s architectural critic Paul Goldberger offered this thought:

> *When companies plan wildly ambitious, over-the-top headquarters, it is sometimes a sign of imperial hubris. A.T. & T. was broken up not too long after it moved into Johnson and Burgee's famously grandiose*

"Chippendale skyscraper" on Madison Avenue. General Foods did not last too long after taking occupancy of the glass-and-metal palace Kevin Roche designed for it in Westchester County, and Union Carbide fell apart after it moved into another Roche building in Danbury, Connecticut. The New York Times Company's stock price plummeted after it moved into its Renzo Piano building on Eighth Avenue, and they now lease the home they built for themselves.

Figure 3.2 Citigroup Center

Architecture isn't in itself a cause of corporate decline—that notion is ridiculous—but overbearing buildings can sometimes be a symptom of companies losing touch with reality, and this problem will manifest itself in other ways."[3]

Such as in corporate aircraft and even executive birthday parties.

Although in some things "the more the merrier" is a positive, to me new model corporate aircraft fleets and lavish parties are both real-time warning signs. Confidence is one thing. Self-assured certainty is another thing altogether.

The Peak in Gold?

A great recent example of an investment with an easy to understand Big Truth was gold. The radio ads all but spelled it out for investors as announcers emphasized how the precious metal was "a hedge against both inflation and deflation" and how it served "as a store of value in a world of fiat (paper) currencies and volatile markets."

What I found so interesting, though, was how the market's confidence in gold began to be translated to decision making that reflected greater and greater permanence as to gold's value as the price of gold kept moving higher. In February 2011, for example, after a two-year doubling in price, *The Wall Street Journal* reported that J.P. Morgan had begun to accept gold as collateral for other commodity and financing transactions, noting that "By making the

---

[3] Paul Goldberger, "Apple's New Headquarters," *The New Yorker*, September 20, 2011, www.newyorker.com/online/blogs/newsdesk/2011/09/apple-new-headquarters.html.

announcement, J.P. Morgan [was] effectively saying gold is as rock solid an investment as triple-A rated Treasuries, adding to a movement that places gold at the top tier of asset classes."[4]

To me this was akin to the now-viewed-as-irrational boom in home equity lending at the very top of the housing market, in which borrowers could easily monetize the equity in their rapidly appreciating homes. I thought *The Wall Street Journal*'s characterization of gold as "rock solid an investment as triple-A rated Treasuries" too was telling, particularly as not six months later U.S. Treasuries were no longer triple-A!

But there were other warning signs for a significant peak in gold as well. Ads in our local paper from companies offering to buy gold grew from quarter page to two or three full pages from more and more competing companies. Local store fronts were suddenly being replaced by "Cash for Gold" operations, many run by people who appeared to know little about the underlying risks of such businesses. All that the new owners saw was opportunity.

What I found particularly interesting about the bubble in gold, however, was that fear and greed were truly indistinguishable. Depending on with whom you spoke they were either investing because they thought others would want or need gold, or they were buying it to protect themselves from falling markets elsewhere. Everyone had a Big Truth.

---

[4] Carolyn Cui and Rhiannon Hoyle, "J.P. Morgan Will Accept Gold as Type of Collateral," *The Wall Street Journal*, February 8, 2011, http://online.wsj.com/article/SB100014240527487044222045761301924 57252596.html.

At the end, though, what really got my attention were comments on Minyanville.com when my friend Todd Harrison, the CEO, posted a column in August 2011 in which he shared that it looked to him like gold was a peaking bubble. The hostility that he received in readers' comments was nothing like I had seen before. The reaction wasn't just middle school; it was middle school on a rampage!

Now, whether or not August 2011 was *the* top or just a very significant top I'll admit I don't know (from its peak in August to its December 2011 low, gold fell by more than 20%), but to me all of the indicators were present: a saturating belief in a Big Truth, hubris-filled self-assured certainty, naïve novice entrants, and credit extension that assumed higher and higher prices. To top it all off—and to my point about fear and greed being indistinguishable— timed to near-perfection at the August peak, Venezuelan President Hugo Chavez announced that he wanted all of that country's gold that had been held physically outside of his country—99 tons!—immediately shipped home.

To me that may go down in social mood history as one of the best real-time indicators ever.

Why Investment Peaks Are Different

One of the problems with peaks in mood is that ultimately the overreaching that Jim Collins identified inevitably happens and the self-assured certainty becomes obvious. At that point, the Big Truth is no longer true; and as peaks coincide with saturation, there are no incremental investors to hold up the investment or market that is topping.

Initially those participating in the investment suggest that price declines are buying opportunities and that the problems are "contained." But they rarely, if ever, are. One of the aspects of investment peaks that I believe investors repeatedly fail to appreciate is that there is an entirely different pricing dynamic for assets purchased for their fundamental utility value versus assets purchased for their investment potential. As Bob Prechter writes in his book, *The Wave Principle of Human Social Behavior*:

> It is universally presumed that the primary law of **economics**, i.e., that price is a function of supply and demand, also rules **finance**. However, human behavior with respect to prices of investments is, in a crucial way, the **opposite** of that with respect to prices of goods and services. When the price of a good or service rises, fewer people buy it, and when its price falls, more people buy it. This response allows pricing to keep supply and demand in balance. In contrast, when the price of an investment rises, more people buy it, and when the price falls, fewer people buy it. This behavior is not an occasional financial market anomaly; it always happens.[5]

What makes this principle so important to me is that it creates a situation at the peak where the cost basis for most investors is much closer to the peak price than people realize. This means that even a modest price decline has a high likelihood of rapidly turning profit into loss for a large group of investors. It also means that following a peak in confidence and price, as confidence drops and prices decline, so too will investor demand. On their own, lower prices won't draw investors back. Prices will fall until confidence ultimately

---

[5] Robert R. Prechter, Jr. *The Wave Principle of Human Social Behavior* (Gainesville, Georgia: New Classics Library, 1999) p. 393.

bottoms. I come back to this point when I discuss housing in the next chapter, but I cannot emphasize this point enough, particularly when coupled with my earlier comments regarding credit. At the top you not only see buyers paying top dollar, but their purchases frequently reflect maximum leverage, too. This sets up a high likelihood that not only will buyers lose their entire investment, but lenders will also experience a far greater severity of loss than they (and their regulators) anticipate.

After the Peak

As I hope you can appreciate, the confluence of factors that define a peak naturally also set up a painful aftermath for investors. Big Truths become false. The abdications of risk management become obvious. Complexity becomes unmanageable. The naïve and novice feel betrayed. And overborrowing becomes evident. The illusion embodied in self-assured certainty is broken; and depending on the magnitude of the peak, it is as if we've all learned that there is no Santa Claus. Try as hard as we can, after we don't believe, we simply can't find a way to believe again—at least not without a long passage of time. Lower prices don't help.

But appreciate, too, that following the "all of us, everywhere, forever" attitude that accompanies peak mood, there is a natural migration toward "me, here, now." With it comes increased scrutiny, a further reduction in trust, and so on. We witnessed this firsthand in 2008 with the banking crisis.

From my perspective, this combination of the natural aftermath of overreaching and the migration toward "me, here, now" coupled with our physiological self-protective instincts is what causes bear markets to fall more quickly than bull markets rise.

Final Thoughts

Peaks in confidence are truly a beauty to behold, particularly extreme peaks, with their saturating self-assured certainty and overreaching, and all of the naturally accompanying behaviors that go along with them all reflecting "hopeful delusion."

Still, given our natural bias toward certainty, it is important to recognize that peaks in confidence and "hopeful delusion" can go on longer than you think would be possible. Unlike bottoms in confidence, which tend to be "V" shaped (for reasons I talk about in Chapter 6, "Signs of a Bottom in Social Mood"), peaks in investments (other than commodities—which I also address is Chapter 6) are much more rounded. Peaks are a process in which confidence is tested over and over before investors ultimately concede that they were suffering from "hopeful delusion."

Not to single out Federal Reserve Chairman Ben Bernanke, but I think his own choice of the word "contained" (which he used early on in the mortgage/banking crisis to describe the magnitude of the problems he saw in the subprime mortgage space) captures perfectly how most investors see risks at major peaks. At very high confidence levels, every problem or issue can be contained.

The result is that at major peaks you will see retest after retest in which market participants seem to be asking "Are you really sure?" over and over. So long as the answer remains "Yes," and confidence continues to build, prices will move higher. When confidence begins to fall, however, and there is doubt, prices can quickly turn down.

Again, though, the result is a peaking *process* in which you can literally see the change from rising to falling confidence begin to test investors' conviction.

Before looking at the other end of the confidence spectrum—self-assured uncertainty and market bottoms—I'd like to pause to look at two specific markets: housing and higher education. Through the framework I've just presented, you should be able to better see how all the necessary ingredients aligned to create the near-perfect bubble in housing and why the sector has been so unresponsive to public policy efforts to revive it. Then I take on higher education and answer whether it is or is not the bubble others suggest.

4

A Social Mood Journey Back Through the Housing Bubble

Now that I've presented what I believe are the attributes that consistently reflect the self-assured certainty that accompanies market peaks, let's specifically look at the real estate market and the U.S. housing bubble that topped in 2005.

Although the exponential moves in home builder stocks from 2000 to 2005 suggest that the housing bubble and the dot.com bubble were both similar short-term phenomena, I think it is much more helpful to consider 2000 through 2005 as the culminating "melt up" of a much, much longer bullish cycle in housing that began at the end of the Great Depression.

I offer this distinction because few investors today tend to look at very long cyclical patterns of behavior. While that is to be expected, particularly after the kind of 20-year period of extraordinary technological innovation and market volatility we have experienced (not to mention our current "me, here, now" view of most things), I think that in the case of housing, the more than 70-year bull market is extremely important for several reasons.

First, I think it is safe to say that if you had talked to home-owners at the end of the Great Depression you would have heard almost unequivocally that they viewed their homes as shelter—a roof over their heads, necessary to keep the elements out—and little more.

I note this thought because it suggests to me that at the bottom there was likely to have been a supply-and-demand relationship for housing based on homes' fundamental "utility value." People bought homes for shelter (likely with concerns about the cost of maintenance) with little regard for a home's future investment value. (In fact, I suspect that at the bottom with its accompanying self-assured uncertainty, if there was a long-term view on home prices it was toward lower, not higher prices.)

For this reason, it should be easy to see why, as part of its efforts to stabilize the financial markets the Federal government would have decided to provide price support to the housing market through programs such as FHA and Fannie Mae, both of which were established during the 1930s.

But consider for a moment how our attitude toward housing has changed since the 1930s. During the 1950s, homeownership morphed into a proxy for the achievement of the prosperity of the American Dream and a means by which public policymakers could objectively measure the economic growth of the American middle class.

I don't think it is too much of a stretch to suggest that as a result, prices began to reflect not just housing's utility value, but also its status value. Also note that during this same period Fannie Mae moved first from being a pure federal agency to "a mixed-ownership corporation" (with the government retaining a preferred stock investment in the entity) and then to a completely public company in 1968. After it was public, Fannie Mae began to purchase not just government guaranteed mortgages but also unguaranteed, or private, mortgages (which, even today, are considered to be more risky than government guaranteed mortgages). And to make sure that there was even greater demand and price competition for mortgages, Congress even introduced a competitor to Fannie Mae, Freddie Mac, in 1970.

I would encourage you to pause here to appreciate how growing confidence over the period from after the Second World War through the late 1960s manifested itself with higher demand, higher prices, reduced regulation, and the perception of lower risk (both financial and political). Home-ownership as a necessary ingredient for the achievement of the American Dream created a virtuous public/private sector partnership in which everyone appeared to benefit.

Modern Housing Finance

During the late 1970s, though, high inflation and high mortgage rates took their toll on housing. The industry responded by creating mortgage-backed securities that—first using loans guaranteed by Ginnie Mae and then using private loans backed by Fannie Mae and Freddie Mac—enabled banks and other companies to originate loans and sell them off to other investors whose investment horizons and funding stability were better matched to long duration mortgages. So long as banks and mortgage companies met the agencies' strict loan underwriting criteria, they were able to create a highly efficient business model in which they were paid to originate and service mortgages while interest rate and credit risk were transferred to others. (During the late 1970s and early 1980s as investors became more and more comfortable with the interest rate and credit risk associated with mortgages, underwriters then began slicing the underlying cash flows of pools of mortgages by both credit and duration as well.)

In the 1990s, higher home prices took the industry in two additional directions. As affordability became a public policy concern, under Presidents George H.W. Bush and Bill Clinton, the agencies were encouraged to expand the breadth of mortgages, which they purchased and guaranteed, to include more low- and middle-income homeowners. At the same time, with many homeowners' nest eggs literally tied up in the appreciated value of their homes, banks began offering home equity loans, lines of credit, and reverse mortgages that enabled borrowers to use their homes as collateral for everything from college tuition to vacations.

Again, I encourage you to consider what all of these efforts across the public and private sectors said about our collective confidence in home prices. Appreciate, too, what these efforts did to boost the economy. The virtuous cycle spun faster and faster. Thanks to the "wealth effect" I discussed earlier (see Figure 2.4), more and more Americans saw the capital in their homes (see Figure 4.1) as a permanent element of their wealth and they borrowed and spent accordingly.

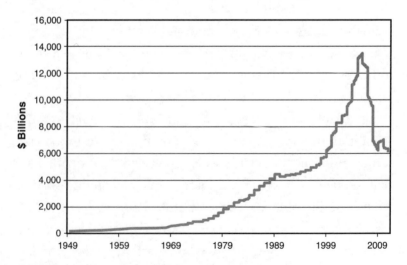

Figure 4.1 Owners' equity in household real estate
Source: Board of Governors of the Federal Reserve System

I think it is important to point out yet another factor providing support to the housing market: falling interest rates (Figure 4.2). With housing affordability not only a function of absolute price, but also of monthly payment levels, the decline in interest rates, even with rising home prices, enabled more Americans to buy homes and existing homeowners to trade up to even larger homes while keeping their monthly payments flat.

CBOE Interest Rate 10-Year T-No

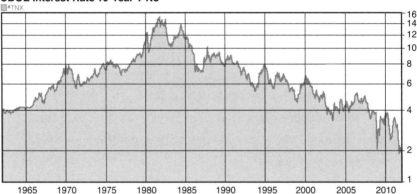

Figure 4.2 Ten-year U.S. Treasury yields

Source: Yahoo! (chart) /CSI (data). Reproduced with permission of Yahoo! Inc.
© 2012 Yahoo! Inc. YAHOO! and the YAHOO! logo are registered trademarks of Yahoo! Inc.

Needless to say, by 2000 the housing flywheel was already spinning very fast. What followed, though, formed the "Perfect Dream" (as opposed to "Perfect Storm") as all of the usual elements of peak mood were aligned with a precipitous decline in nominal mortgage rates.

So using the peak mood "elements" from Chapter 3, "Market Peaks and All the Red Flags They Wave," let's look at the housing market as it soared from 2000 to 2005.

A Big Truth

First, the Big Truth, which had morphed from "homes as shelters" in the Great Depression to "homes as the embodiment of the American Dream" during the 1950s and 1960s, became unequivocally, "homes are a risk-free investment." TV shows like *Flip That House* made that clear to us every night.

I think it is important to appreciate, though, that the Big Truth of "homes as a risk-free investment" came not at the beginning of the bull market in housing that began in the Great Depression, but at the very tail end of it. We saw homes as a risk-free investment because we had the necessary history to support it. Because it had been true, we believed it to be true and we saw it as being true well into the future. Once again, we used the rearview mirror, not the windshield, to see what was ahead.

Please appreciate, too, that with the migration of the Big Truth to "homes as a risk-free investment" also came the "utility" to "investment" shift in supply and demand mechanics. The higher the price of homes went, the more people bought them. American homeownership peaked in 2005.

Abdication of Risk Management

Not surprisingly, the Big Truth of "homes as a risk-free investment" also had a dramatic effect on the second element of peak mood—the abdication of risk management. From loan underwriting standards to the proliferation of second mortgages and home equity lines to investors' blind

reliance on the rating agencies, every step along the mortgage origination conveyor belt reflected an unprecedented
confidence that home values could not and would not
decline. Just consider the chart in Figure 4.3 of revolving
home equity loan balances and what these loans said about
the level of certainty both lenders and borrowers had in
future home values. From 2000 to 2006 balances rose more
than four-fold!

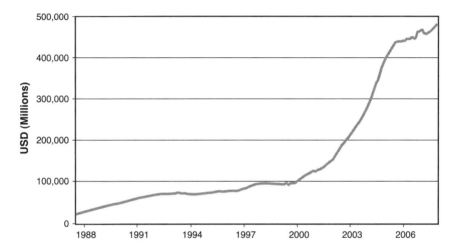

Figure 4.3 Revolving home equity loan balances
Source: Board of Governors of the Federal Reserve System

To me, the clearest measure of the abdication of risk
management, though, can be found in the chart in Figure 4.4
from the Center for Community Capital at UNC.

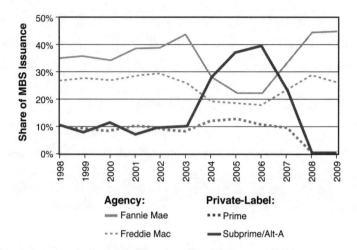

Figure 4.4 1998-2009 mortgage-backed securities issuance

Source: Kevin Park (2010), "Fannie, Freddie and the Foreclosure Crisis," Center for Community Capital, University of North Carolina at Chapel Hill. Data source: Inside Mortgage Finance.

Note how at the very peak of the housing bubble (2005/2006), mortgage-backed securities investors no longer needed guarantees from Fannie Mae and Freddie Mac at all to get comfortable with the underlying credit risk. And even more, within the private-label (non-agency-guaranteed) category itself while "prime" mortgage demand rose, at the top of the market, there was an explosion in lower credit quality Alt-A and lowest quality subprime mortgages.

Organizational Complexity

Then there is the third peak mood element: organization complexity. At the risk of suggesting that a picture is worth a thousand words, I think the chart by Daniel Edstrom of DTC Systems (Figure 4.5), of his family's own mortgage—from application through to funding and then the loan's sale and securitization—offers a far better view of how complicated the mortgage market was at the very top than anything I could possibly write.

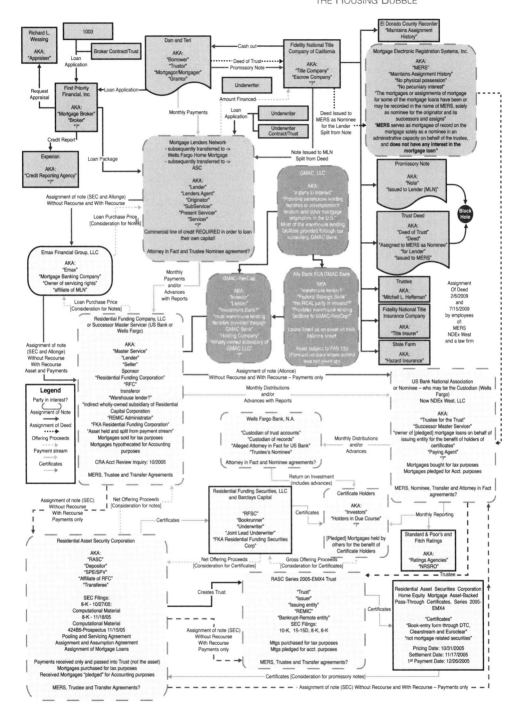

Figure 4.5 Peak complexity in the mortgage industry

Source: Daniel Edstrom, DTC Systems

Further, note how this complexity was not only exacer-
bated by the abdication of risk management at the very top,
but also how it also lent itself to fraudulent behavior, especially given the peak in trust that naturally accompanied the
very top. The fact that the mortgage industry is now subject
to record litigation should be a surprise to no one, particularly
when you consider the number of participants and transactions involved.

Novice and Naïve Entrants

Given what I am sure were the truly well-intentioned
bipartisan public policy objectives of broadening homeownership to include more lower and middle class Americans, the
fourth peak mood element of novice and naïve entrants was
not just satisfied, but all but mandated, by Washington policymakers. Thanks to the abdication of risk management by
both lenders and regulators, most often these borrowers were
paired with low introductory rate mortgages, which, because
of the collapse in short-term rates following 9/11, made housing appear to be affordable for the first time to an entirely
new low-credit-score segment of the market. Unfortunately,
because credit defaults from the peak—when underwriting
criteria are the weakest—backward, these buyers have been
the most adversely affected by the housing bubble's collapse.
The same is true for the buyers of most subprime mortgage
securities, who like the borrowers themselves were also the
last to participate.

As noted earlier, by the peak in 2005 American homeownership had risen to a record of almost 70%. In contrast,
at the bottom of the Great Depression, the figure stood at

just 43.6%—a point I return to later in the book. At the top, I think it is safe to say that everyone who could buy a home had.

Excessive Credit and Architecture

Needless to say, the final two peak mood elements of excessive credit and opulent, self-aggrandizing architecture are today all too obvious. The term *McMansion* has even entered our vernacular. Once again self-assured certainty led to the overreaching that Jim Collins warned about, and in the case of housing it was a self-assured certainty that saturated all participants across the private and public sectors.

Hopefully, though, when looked at in the context of a time frame of more than 70 years it is easier to see how light goes to dark, not overnight, but through the thousands of shades of darker and darker gray that naturally accompany greater and greater confidence. Still, when held up to the objective criteria that accompany peak mood, it is difficult for me to see how both the private and public sectors missed the peaking of the housing bubble, particularly as we were literally building it in our own backyards.

That is the nature of peaks in mood. By the time the peak hits, Big Truths are so firmly ingrained and so fundamentally black or white that to suggest that the future won't follow the past is, I am afraid, to fundamentally question whether night will continue to follow day. To me, though, that is why investors must constantly challenge what they are most certain of, particularly when this certainty is shared by all others.

Final Thoughts

To be clear, what I have just offered on the housing bub-ble represents a "best of" application of the major elements of peak confidence. For every element, there is much more that could have been written with example after example capable of filling a book all to itself. As I offered earlier, at the peak, there is a saturation of self-assured certainty across the entire food chain. This chapter is only the "highlights tour."

Still, it is remarkable how few people believed that hous-ing was a bubble at the top. That is the nature of the social vor-tex that accompanies self-assured certainty. We all believed.

Today, we all know that housing was a bubble. Because it's been more than six years since the peak, I have the lux-ury of writing about the housing bubble with the clarity only afforded by hindsight.

Rather than taking another burst bubble through my peak mood criteria with the benefit of hindsight, though, in the next chapter I objectively evaluate something else that is now the source of near-constant debate: whether higher educa-tion is a bubble.

5

Is Higher Education a Bubble?

Recently there has been a flurry of opinion pieces written about higher education that argue both pro and con that, like housing, higher education is also a bubble.

Although the arguments could fill a book all to itself, in this chapter I use the peak mood framework from Chapter 3, "Market Peaks and All the Red Flags They Wave," to assess whether higher education qualifies as a bubble.

A Big Truth

Much like homeownership became a measurable standard of the achievement of the American Dream during the 1950s, so did earning a college diploma, especially with the introduction of the GI Bill after the end of the Second World War. Consequently, the cost of college became the necessary "investment in the future" that would translate into a better job and job security, a high probability of homeownership, and a secure retirement. Put simply, with a college degree the future was more certain.

Two things strike me as important in our cultural definition of college tuition as an "investment in the future." First, I would not underestimate how as an *investment in the future* we naturally want more of it (like all other investments) at higher and higher prices. Despite the recent concerns about the value of a college education the data clearly suggests that per capita enrollment has been rising right alongside rising tuition.[1]

Second, like many of the recent mantras regarding gold, fear and greed are all but indistinguishable for most when it comes to paying college tuition. We pay ever rising tuition to both avoid a painful downside—the lack of a good job (fear)—and to obtain a positive upside—the opportunity for a better paying job (greed). Although some may suggest these are merely the opposite sides of the same coin, we shouldn't underestimate the effect this has on the demand for higher education. (In this regard note that the increasing emphasis by public policymakers on the *"importance* of education" is not at all dissimilar to the comments of gold advertisers about the *importance* of holding gold in one's investment portfolio as both a hedge against inflation and deflation.)

From my perspective, higher education's Big Truth makes it clear that like any investment there is an opportunity for a bubble in its price. Even more, with our willingness to pay for higher education largely a function of our perception of college's ability to make our future (or our children's or grandchildren's future) more certain, it is also easy to see how self-assured certainty could set in and how we could ultimately find ourselves in a state of hopeful delusion, particularly, if like housing, we have had a long track record of success that demonstrates higher education's value. Further, we should not underestimate the role that parents, teachers,

---

[1] Alan Hall, "Back to the School of Hard Knocks?" *The Socionomist* (February 2011): 1-2.

and others in the workforce play in the college process. Because college made their own lives more certain, parents and friends extrapolate their own success to those considering college. While clearly well-intentioned, this is not that dissimilar from a long-term investor recommending that you buy Apple stock because he or she has already made a lot of money in it. What parents and friends may think is a forward-looking "windshield" for a college-bound student, I am afraid may actually be their own "rear view mirror."

Finally, I want to point out the clearly black-or-white nature of the investment premise of higher education. College either does or does not make one's future more certain. From a perception standpoint, there is no middle ground. But please appreciate that without commensurate wage growth, the higher tuition prices rise, the further out into the future prospective students must think they see that certainty and the clear financial benefits of college. (Or, to put it in financial terms, is the cost of higher education greater or less than the present value of the future certainty we perceive that arises from college? That is to say, is there a positive net present value [NPV]?)

So long as social mood is rising and Horizon Preference is expanding, none of this is a problem. Any concern about higher tuition costs is mitigated by the increased perception of greater certainty in the future that accompanies growing confidence. The problem comes, though, when social mood deteriorates. At that point, time horizons shrink and rather than focusing on college as an investment to be recouped over, say, 10, 20, or even 40 years, students instead are likely to look to see whether they will be able to get a job upon graduation—a dramatic shrinking of the time horizon! Even worse, the reality of having paid top dollar (and borrowing to do so) imposes not only an enormous financial burden, but also a psychological one as well. As a result, current graduates are likely to feel the same kind of betrayal that many home-owners now do.

I highlight this because should the Big Truth of higher education fail to be true, the consequences are likely to be significant and long lasting for the entire higher education industry.

So does the Big Truth suggest that the peak is here? I think so. The amount of certainty—and, more importantly, the time horizon of that extreme certainty—that prospective students must now have about the future benefits arising from their degree in order to justify college's high tuition (and the associated student loan burdens—on average more than $25,000 for every college graduate) today appears to be, well, self-assured. And needless to say, that defines the top.

Abdication of Risk Management

Although I am sure few, if any, college boards would agree, looking objectively at the financial model for most colleges today, it is hard not to see an abdication of risk management. From my perspective, there is an enormous mismatch today between colleges' social mood/confidence-dependent revenue sources and their fixed expense bases. On the expense side of the ledger, there are large fixed costs arising from both tenured faculty and extensive physical facilities and on the other side there are significant social mood-driven revenues—particularly donor giving, endowment revenue, tuition and for public universities, as discussed below, state funding.

Admittedly, many universities got a short-term taste of this mismatch during 2008 when their endowment values fell sharply, but there was no material decline in enrollment, and, for most schools, donor giving has quickly rebounded along with the stock market. As a result, the mismatch was quickly "contained" and few institutions from my perspective have seriously considered the potential for a sustained concurrent drop in enrollment, giving, and endowment values.

But there are other revenue/expense mismatches that I think colleges have also ignored. Sports-related revenues clearly align with rising and falling confidence levels, whereas the underlying costs, particularly facility costs, remain largely fixed. For most public institutions, the same is also true for state and federal funding, which largely ebbs and flows on tax receipts, another clear social mood/confidence connector.

If you believe as I do that confidence and market levels are correlated, then the net result is that higher education revenues are much, much more correlated to the market than those in the industry perceive today. Few schools, if any, have done anything to mitigate this clear enterprise risk.

Social Mood, Philanthropy, and Food for Thought for Non-Profits

Although this chapter focuses specifically on higher education, I think it is important for individuals and organizations involved directly with philanthropy and charitable giving to appreciate the tight correlation of generosity with social mood and the markets. Put simply, a donor's willingness to give is tied far more to his or her own level of confidence than it is to the severity of the need of the recipient.

From my perspective most not-for-profit organizations, particularly those involved with social needs, woefully underestimate how leveraged they truly are to the market/social mood. In good times not only do rising markets boost these groups' endowments and lift donor giving, it often lessens the social need itself. (For example, rising employment levels lead to a declining need for food banks and other social services.) On the other hand, the decline in market prices that accompanies falling mood depletes endowments at a time when donor contributions are likely to be falling and the mission-related needs of the organization are rising.

Some organizations have tried to mitigate this risk by relying on portfolio diversification in their endowments and calculating their annual endowment draws using a three-, five- or even ten-year rolling average. To me, most organizations would be far better off considering an enterprise-wide assessment of their social mood-related risks and to use their endowments' asset allocation to help manage and, in most cases, mitigate that risk.

Rather than the 60/40 equity to fixed income mix that many endowments deploy, I suspect that most would be much better served by an allocation that is at a minimum the reverse. That said, I'd also throw out the thought that by the time most organizations finally come to this conclusion, their own risk-averse behavior (and their willingness—if not outright eagerness—to sacrifice more potential market appreciation in exchange for greater loss protection) is likely to accompany a major bottoming of the markets.

Organizational Complexity

From the unbridled expansion of graduate programs and "global" campuses (in "exotic" locales no less) to the proliferation of customized and integrated degree programs, American universities have followed the financial services industry in the belief that they can deliver all programs to all students anywhere. But oddly enough, whereas customization abounds, automation at most institutions is an anathema. Most tenured faculty on American campuses struggle with the idea that they can be more efficient, and only a small number of colleges have eagerly embraced the potential offered by online education. It is an industry that is struggling to reconcile hand-crafted tradition with a new technology age.

Naïve and Novice Participants

Although those in the for-profit higher education industry might find this comment objectionable, I see this segment as having many of the same fundamental characteristics of the subprime mortgage industry—a late arrival to a well-entrenched industry; reliant on naïve/novice participants; extremely reliant on debt (particularly government debt); a heavy sales dominated corporate culture; and so on.

From my perspective, the fact that many for-profit institutions began to melt down in 2010 was a significant "early warning" sign for the entire higher education industry. Yes, to date it has been "contained," but the similarities to housing suggest that rather than being the only segment of higher education to experience hardship, it is merely the first.

And here the reaction to the plight of the for-profit colleges by most established colleges is also very telling. Like prime mortgage lenders at the beginning of the mortgage crisis, well-established colleges have been very dismissive, suggesting that their own American colleges and universities are clearly *not* in the same category as the online, for-profit schools. That may be the case, but I am afraid that in the process of celebrating the current hardships of the for-profit education industry, the higher education establishment is both ignoring the real risks to their own models due to deteriorating social mood and the potential for new entrants, like Khan Academy, to offer innovative, low cost, if not free, alternative solutions online.

Excessive Credit

As I write this, student loan debt in this country alone has topped $1.0 trillion, exceeding the balance of credit card debt by more than 30%. As significant as this balance is, however, it ignores the amount of unreported college-related debt that families took on during the 1990s and early 2000s using the equity of their homes as collateral. Totaled together, the figure for outstanding college-related debt on the books of students, parents, and grandparents is probably between $1.5 and $2.0 trillion. And that estimate could be low.

With most private sources drying up after the banking crisis in 2008, the Federal government stepped in to close the gap. But note the trajectory of U.S. government consumer debt (substantially all of which is related to student loans) in Figure 5.1. As economist Herb Stein said, "If something cannot go on forever, it will stop." With the average graduate now leaving college with more than $25,000 in student loan debt, I think we have reached or will soon rapidly reach the point where the willingness and ability of students to borrow money for college and the willingness and ability of the U.S. government to lend it to students has topped.

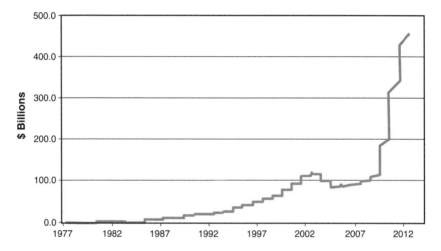

Figure 5.1 Total consumer loans by federal government
Source: Board of Governors of the Federal Reserve System

As noted earlier, lending and borrowing reflect confidence. In the case of student loans, that level of confidence feels more like self-assured certainty to me.

Architecture

As a parent of a soon-to-be-graduating high school student, I have had several chances recently to tour the architectural element of the peak mood in higher education first hand. (And if there were any lingering doubts as to the true social mood connections between the financial markets and higher education, a listing of donor names over the doors of new buildings on America's campuses would all but eliminate it.)

But to those who might be wondering whether this architectural correlation between mood and the markets on campus is new, let me offer the chart in Figure 5.2 of the new buildings/facilities constructed at my alma mater, the College of William and Mary, and the Dow Jones Industrial Average since 1900.[2]

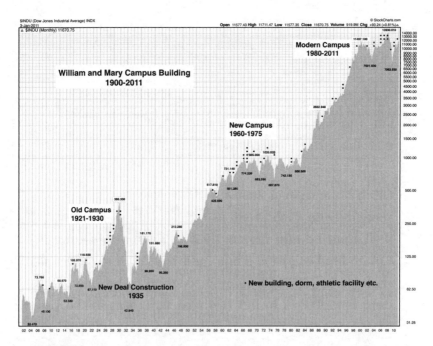

Figure 5.2 New building construction at the College of William and Mary, 1900 to today

Source: Stockcharts (Dow Jones Industrial Average chart)

[2] I would like to acknowledge the invaluable assistance of Louise Kale, college historian of the College of William and Mary, for her help on this chart. Building-specific data from The Special Collections Research Center (SCRC) Wiki of the Swem Library (http://scrc.swem.wm.edu/wiki/index.php/Category:College_of_William_and_Mary_Buildings).

With few exceptions, the major buildings/facilities on campus all tie to major market peaks—the late 1920s, the late 1960s/early 1970s and 2000 and 2007. But I would note that there is a significant distinction between the most recent building boom and the other two major construction periods from the past century. In the earlier building "booms" there were major academic buildings constructed that were followed near the very top of the market with more "student-centered" buildings, such as more spacious dormitories, improved athletic facilities, and so on. In fact William and Mary opened its "Sorority Court" in September 1929.

What is significant to me is the large number of facilities built over the past 20 years on William and Mary's campus—and judging by my own visits, on other college campuses as well—that go well beyond supporting the core undergraduate academic program. Most building activity was to support expanding graduate programs, student activities, athletics, and the arts—what we saw at the very top of prior confidence cycles. I would feel much more optimistic about the prospects for the higher education industry if what was constructed on campus was more "mission critical." My concern is that what we have witnessed is the McMansion'ing of college campuses—just as we saw at the peak of the housing market in suburbia—with colleges adding high-cost, nice-to-have facilities based on an extreme level of self-assured certainty.

Final Thoughts

Like the previous chapter on the housing bubble, I have tried to highlight just a few of the major themes that I see in higher education and how they tie to the elements that naturally accompany peaks in social mood. In fairness, a more thorough review would require a book all to itself.[3]

Whether higher education is in a bubble only time will tell, but using the peak mood characteristics exhibited in other investment bubbles, there are certainly plenty of similarities to be concerned about.

My intent is that by looking at the experience of the housing industry and the current state of higher education, you have a better sense of how extremes in confidence alter decision making and how we naturally choose "us, everywhere, forever" solutions at the top.

Still, I am afraid that, like those in the housing industry before them, higher education leaders today don't yet grasp what being on the other side of an investment bubble means. Education is not a utility good that can be fixed simply by better aligning supply and demand. Lower tuition won't bring greater enrollment, and unlike housing, there is no "rental" investor to sop up excess supply as prices decline.

For the established American university system, it is at risk of a devastating one-two punch in which a decline in social mood is also accompanied by a concurrent revolutionary change in technology. The system is akin to the newspaper industry circa 2000. From my perspective, education leaders and public policy makers would be wise to look at the recent experiences of residential housing and print media as they consider the road ahead. Both examples highlight the significant leadership challenges of managing through

---

[3] A great middle ground, for those looking for an excellent socionomic analysis of higher education, is Alan Hall's article, "Back to the School of Hard Knocks?," in the February 2011 *The Socionomist*. Alan's detailed review brings in many more examples and looks at American higher education over a much longer time frame.

profound deflationary change and, in the case of housing, the limits of traditional public policy solutions in the aftermath of an investment bubble.

Having looked at peaks of confidence in concept and through the examples of residential real estate and higher education, in the next chapter, I turn to the other end of the mood spectrum and look at the behavioral characteristics of self-assured uncertainty that accompany extreme lows in confidence and market bottoms.

6

Signs of a Bottom in Social Mood

During the 2008 banking crisis, David Rosenberg, then chief economist of Merrill Lynch (and now chief economist of Gluskin Sheff), offered, "Bear markets don't end in hope; they end in despair." I held on to this quote because it ran counter to what I believed at the time and to what I believe most investors still think. Yet it's all too true. If self-assured certainty and overreaching are experienced at the top, then self-assured uncertainty, along with a dire sense of futility and hopelessness, must accompany the bottom.

You would think then that the characteristics of bottoms in social mood and confidence would simply be the opposite of what we witness at the top; that Big Truths would instead be seen as Big Lies; that instead of an abdication of risk management, there would be a near-coronation of it; that complexity would be replaced by simplicity; that novice and naïve entrants would have completely exited and that the only ones left standing would be long-time, experienced, and sophisticated participants; that excessive credit would be replaced by excessive equity and a complete unwillingness to borrow and lend; and that instead of constructing new buildings, we would instead be tearing them down.

All of these opposite elements are in fact true characteristics of a bottom, but I am afraid that they don't quite capture the real essence as to why that would be the case.

Extreme "Me, Here, Now" Behaviors

As I noted at the beginning of the book, bottoms in confidence reflect not only uncertainty, but self-assured uncertainty. To borrow Dave's line from this chapter's introduction, at the bottom despair reigns and there is an omnipresent sense that we don't know what, if any, good the future will bring. It is a state of fear-filled delusion that we see as a long-lasting, if not permanent, condition.

The net result, though, is that our decisions and actions reflect extreme "me, here, now" choices. At the bottom generosity is replaced with selfishness and self-interested behavior as it is *my*, not *our*, survival that matters most to me. In addition, what was once viewed as offering permanent certainty—such as wealth and income—is now not only temporary, but even the time span of temporary is uncertain. It could be a day, a week, or a month. Who knows? At the bottom, I not only believe that the rug may be pulled out from under me, but I have come to expect it. What happens on a national, let alone international level, is also almost meaningless to me. As I noted in Chapter 1, "Understanding Social Mood," when we are most fearful our worlds are very small. Everything is local and we want the people and things that are most important to us to be close—extremely close.

Having reflected on self-assured uncertainty for some time, I believe that better than any of the "opposite" elements I listed, perhaps the best characteristics of a trough in confidence can be captured in the words "hoarding" and "sacrifice."

Before discussing both of these traits, let me reinforce that like the saturated sensation of self-assured certainty that we feel at the top, at the very bottom there is an equivalent sensation of saturating self-assured uncertainty. That is to say that there is a consistent "all-in" or "all-out" sentiment that is shared. Again, and importantly, it is shared up and down the entire food chain. For a specific company, not only must investors feel self-assured uncertainty regarding the future prospects of the company, but so too must suppliers, creditors, analysts, managers, and so on. All must feel a sense of hopelessness. (And, in light of current events in Europe, let me note here that these same characteristics also apply to countries and governments as well.) If this feels like the moment just before bankruptcy, that is because it often is. In truly extreme troughs, bankruptcy, if not outright liquidation, is what naturally results when there is a saturating collective absence of hope. I hope that by offering this extreme scenario you can get a feeling for the sensation of the mood that accompanies bottoms that I am trying to describe.

Hoarding Behaviors

With that sense of uncertainty in mind, let me turn to hoarding. I suspect that when some of you read the word *hoarding* your minds immediately turned to the runs on the banks experienced in the U.S. during the Great Depression. (And, yes, those runs really did correspond to the extraordinary sense of uncertainty that accompanied the market/social mood bottom.) But I encourage you to think of hoarding much more broadly than just the natural urge to hold physical cash as mood deteriorates and to consider the word in the context of generosity. As mood deteriorates toward the bottom, all aspects of our generosity (financial, social, emotional, political, and so on) toward others drops dramatically. In some extreme cases it even ceases to exist.

When presented in this light, I suggest that it opens a broad range of actions that reflect, for example, that at the bottom there is no benefit of the doubt given. Not surprisingly, at a bottom you often see shareholders replace directors, and boards replace executive leadership. Similarly, you see companies shutter a troublesome business unit or stop manufacturing a supposedly "flawed" product at a trough.

Also note that as markets approach bottoms, governments behave with self-interestedness comparable to the private sector. As do voters at the polls. Extremes in nationalism and isolationism, not to mention regulation and even authoritarianism, are normal natural accompaniments to what is witnessed in the corporate environment during periods of extreme self-assured uncertainty. As public sector actions often receive far more attention in the media than what happens in business, I strongly encourage investors to also consider the nature of major policy decisions in their assessment of mood, particularly in down markets. Again, changes in social mood affect all aspects of the world around us, and there may be no group more reactive to those changes than politicians and public policymakers.

If bear markets end in despair, then at the bottom we act desperately. But what is particularly interesting to me about moments of peak self-assured uncertainty is how our desperate actions are all specifically focused on doing something to end our state of hopelessness. To me this is why investors naturally sell losing stocks at the bottom. With intense hopelessness, there is an acute need to do something—in some cases literally anything—to create a renewed level of certainty. I contrast this to market tops where we want things to go on forever (and certainly want to believe that they will). With bottoms, there is much more of a saturating "Make it stop *right now!*" quality. At the very bottom, we want it to be over immediately.

Commodity Peaks

I realize this may seem like an odd location to discuss peaks in commodities, but I would encourage you to think about these moments as having behavioral attributes much more consistent with market bottoms than market tops. As a rule, commodity peaks accompany a saturating self-assured sense of scarcity—that there is and will continue to be a significant shortage in the specific product. That permanent sense of scarcity (and the resulting hoarding) reflects an extreme "me, here, now" mood.

The consequence is that commodity peaks are typically much more event-like in their formation. Rather than the rounded tops experienced in other markets, commodity peaks are often very sharp-tipped—rapid melt-ups followed by sudden melt-downs. The oil market exhibited this behavior in 2008, and gold followed a similar pattern in 2011.

I am sure for some readers my reference earlier to Venezuelan president Chavez's demand that all of the country's gold holdings be repatriated in mid-August 2011 may have been confusing. Hopefully, now it makes more sense. President Chavez was displaying classic "me, here, now" hoarding behavior.

In commodities, that happens at tops, not bottoms.

But I would also offer that the alignment of the early 1970s gas crisis and the 2008 peak in oil to periods of significant equity market decline/turbulence makes sense. All are reflections of a significant drop in social mood and the natural reactions—and overreactions—to an extreme "me, here, now" environment.

Acts of Sacrifice

Many pundits describe market bottoms as capitulations; but I suggest that rather than throwing in the towel, investors are actually deliberately taking action to end their uncertainty. Just as market tops don't end in complacency, market bottoms don't end in resignation. To me, at the very bottom, investors are prepared to sacrifice any and all potential upside to end their uncertainty and what they see as the real potential (if not outright certainty) for even further downside. (Conversely, at the top, investors eagerly and willfully swap all potential downside to keep their self-assured certainty alive. They overreach.)

For these reasons, I think sacrifice is an important characteristic in the behaviors exhibited at market bottoms. As noted earlier, sometimes that sacrifice is a leader or leadership team of a company whereas at other times it could be a division or a product or product line. In bankruptcy it is obviously creditors' and shareholders' financial interests that are sacrificed. But, again, at the bottom a very deliberate action is being taken to end uncertainty.

There is another important aspect to this as well. To me, hoarding is all about ending the current uncertainty by trying to hold onto and hopefully return to a *past* that you believe to be more certain than the present. Sacrifice, on the other hand, is all about changing the current uncertain present into a more certain *future*. When we sacrifice we acknowledge that we can't go back. We burn the ships; and in doing so we perceive that there will be a better future as a result of our action.

Implicit in sacrifice is a rising level of confidence (otherwise the sacrificial action would not yet have been taken). I realize that this might seem like angels dancing on the head of a pin, but implicit in sacrifice is a critical mind shift from both the past (the more certain past that we believe that through hoarding we can somehow return to) and the present (our current uncertainty) to sometime in the future. That is to say that rather than our Horizon Preference continuing to move to the lower left, embedded in an act of sacrifice is an important reversal in direction back toward the upper right, as shown in Figure 6.1. Further, and I don't mean to overstate this point, but the act of sacrifice frequently involves doing something today to not just change the future for oneself, but for others—generosity, which is another trait of moving toward the upper right.

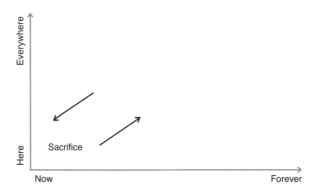

Figure 6.1 Bottoms in social mood reflect acts of sacrifice
Source: Financial Insyghts

Now, some of you might be thinking that sacrifice and hoarding are at opposite ends of the spectrum of behavior, but in the context of eliminating uncertainty I don't think that is at all the case. Both actions reflect an expressed decision to end mounting self-assured uncertainty. As I said earlier, people who hoard are trying to hold on to the past, whereas people who sacrifice are trying to change the future. As we get closer and closer to the bottom in social mood we hoard with ever increasing intensity—and, again, not only financially but in other socially less-generous ways as well. At the very bottom, though, when hoarding fails to be successful and we can't take the uncertainty any more, we act in desperation and we sacrifice.

Social Hoarding and Sacrifice

Earlier in the book, I showed a chart showing the alignment of the riots in London with the bottom of the FTSE 100 in August 2011. While this may make some readers uncomfortable, I suggest that those riots provide a great social example of the often concurrent hoarding/sacrifice behaviors that naturally accompany significant market bottoms. Those still shaking their heads at the relationship between social actions and the markets may want to review the chart in Figure 6.2 from Mark Galasiewski of Elliott Wave International, which plots major terrorism/social unrest events in the Middle East against the Egyptian stock market's HERMES index.

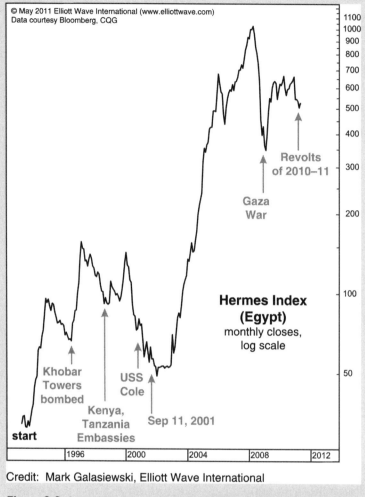

Credit: Mark Galasiewski, Elliott Wave International

Figure 6.2 Acts of terrorism and major bottoms in the market align

Until I saw this chart, I had thought of 9/11 as an event that caused our stock market to fall. Today, I see the horrific event as the result of the kind of action some people are unfortunately willing to make at the bottom of severe declines in social mood and the markets. (And so that you may appreciate the opposite end of the confidence spectrum as well, I would note that the U.S. military operation in Pakistan that resulted in the killing of Osama Bin Laden occurred on May 2, 2011, the same day that U.S. stock market peaked after rising for 26 months and more than 80% from its March 2009 low.)

I hope that the chart also helps to frame the Arab Spring and the sacrificial element implicit in the willingness of individuals along the northern coast of Africa to rise up against their governments. Although I don't pretend to know whether the Arab Spring represents *the* bottom for the Egyptian stock market, what we are witnessing there from a social mood perspective suggests that we are actually much closer to a buying opportunity than it might feel to most readers. That said, you need to seriously consider that even if THE market bottom is in place, your ability to capitalize financially on that opportunity as an investor is hardly assured.

Event Versus Cycle Lows

Having discussed the sensation of saturating self-assured uncertainty and the hoarding and sacrifice aspects that go along with it in concept, I want to look at a few real market/mood bottoms. Before I do that, though, I want to distinguish between what many think of as "event"-driven market bottoms and cyclical lows.

Today, when many investors think of major market bottoms, they associate them with significant events like September 11, 2001, the Lehman Brothers failure in 2008, or even the 1929 crash—dates of violent market declines. Although all of these events, like the 2011 tsunami in Japan, represented trading lows—with significant bounces thereafter—in all cases the markets subsequently moved to lower lows before bottoming.

What is remarkable, though, about the ultimate lows in the market for each of these "events"—in October 2002, March 2009, and even July 1932—is that there is nothing "individually" specific or remarkable about them. There is no single event that puts an exclamation point on why the market bottomed on the specific day that it did.

To me, this speaks to the saturation aspect of market bottoms (and tops, for that matter) in which the ultimate turning point is merely the extreme culmination of mood—like the moment when the very last tile is finally placed into a much more elaborate mosaic.

With that in mind, let's take a look at the actions that occurred during the weeks leading up to the major market lows of 2002, 2009, and 1932.

The Market Low of 2002

During September 2002, as the major indices bottomed, President Bush pressured both Congress and the UN Security Council to draft resolutions to allow for military intervention in Iraq. At the same time there were anti-war protests in major U.S. cities and in London. Senator Robert Torricelli of New Jersey withdrew from his reelection campaign due to ethics issues, and New York State Attorney General Eliot Spitzer filed civil fraud lawsuits against current and former executives of WorldCom, Qwest, Metro Fiber Networks, and McLeod USA. In early October, Washington, DC's "Beltway Sniper" struck for the first time.

But note, too, how in the week following the market bottom, Congress voted to give President Bush war powers to proceed with the Iraq invasion, former President Jimmy Carter was awarded the Nobel Peace Prize, and the nightclub car bombing in Bali occurred. All of these likely reflected decisions that were reached as social mood was bottoming.

Wars and Market Bottoms

Many economists and historians like to suggest that World War II lifted us out of the Great Depression. Note, though, that nobody even suggests today that the Iraq War lifted us out of the market bottom in 2002. I highlight this distinction because in both cases, war reflected the kind of "sacrifice" brought on by the self-assured uncertainty that naturally accompanies market bottoms. Countries don't enter war because they want to. They go to war because they believe they need to change the future into something more certain.

The Market Low of March 2009

During the weeks leading up to the March 2009 low, Swiss banking giant UBS announced that it had settled tax evasion charges with U.S. prosecutors and replaced its CEO. Other major global banks reported staggering fourth quarter 2008 losses and the U.S. government increased its stake in Citigroup to 36%, and the U.K. government raised its stake in Lloyds to more than 60%. New York State Attorney General Andrew Cuomo subpoenaed Bank of America's Chairman and CEO Ken Lewis for misleading investors during the late 2008 purchase of Merrill Lynch. President Obama announced that most U.S. troops would leave Iraq by August 2010 and the American Reconstruction and Reinvestment Act passed Congress. Finally, following CNBC contributor Rick Santelli's on-air rant, the first Tea Party demonstration was held in Chicago, and more than 100,000 people gathered in Dublin to protest Ireland's handling of the financial crisis.

The Decision to Leave Iraq

Note that in March 2009, at the very market bottom, President Obama announced that the U.S. would leave Iraq, the direct opposite presidential decision from October 2002, another major market bottom.

As contradictory as that may seem, I believe that the two reflect the same mood-based decision making. The deep deterioration in social mood, in the aftermath of 9/11, led to the Iraq War because political leaders believed that something needed to be done to end the uncertainty (both economic and related to the threat of terrorism). By going to war, there was a belief that the future would be more certain—and here I would again emphasize that desperate need to do something as mood is bottoming. Just sitting is emotionally paralyzing.

Not seven years after entering Iraq, though, public sentiment had shifted 180 degrees. By the spring of 2009, the Iraq War in the minds of many, particularly political leaders in Washington, equaled uncertainty. By calling for the return of U.S. troops, President Obama believed he was creating a more certain future for the United States.

I can imagine some readers at this point might be reaching for their old stock charts and then noting that President

Nixon announced the end of the Vietnam War on January 23, 1973, just as the markets were peaking ahead of a very precipitous decline.

Wouldn't that directly contradict what happened in Iraq?

Not at all. President Nixon announced the initial troop withdrawals and "Vietnamization" during the bear market of 1969. The January 1973 announcement, on the other hand, was for a culminating peace treaty that followed severe U.S. bombing of Hanoi in December 1972 and was made only after North Vietnam's Le Du Tho agreed to terms with then Secretary of State Dr. Henry Kissinger. It was "peace with honor." Although subsequent events in Vietnam ultimately changed the final outcome, I think it is important to note that the peace treaty reflected a high degree of confidence, certainty, and trust—all characteristics that naturally accompany peaks in social mood.

The Market Bottom of 1932

In looking through newspapers and magazine stories from 1932, what comes across so clearly is the extraordinary self-assuredness of the uncertainty experienced at the bottom of the Great Depression. People were not just uncertain, they were truly certain of being uncertain. Not surprisingly then, their actions during the spring and summer of 1932 reflected the collective culminating desperation of the period: the passage of the Glass-Steagall Act (splitting banks from brokerages, the supposed "culprits" of the 1929 Crash); the kidnapping of the Lindbergh baby; the suicide of the Swedish financier "Match King"; World War I veteran protests in Washington; demands by the Daughters of the American

Revolution for the deportation of jobless aliens; President Hoover's admission that Prohibition was a failure. The feeling of hopelessness was saturating—so much so that in August 1932, the month after the market bottom, for the first time in U.S. history emigration exceeded immigration. (One report noted that "the majority of the immigrants leaving on their own initiative did so anticipating a collapse in their fortunes [had they stayed]."[1])

Seeing Major Market Bottoms in Real Time

Admittedly, the market/mood bottoms that I have just discussed represent the end of three of the most severe declines in social mood/market corrections over the past 80 years, and I have the clear benefit of hindsight in evaluating them. But less severe market troughs offer similar characteristics, just to a lesser degree.

As noted in Chapter 2, "Horizon Preference: How Mood Affects Our Decision Making," the August 2011 market low for the FTSE 100 coincided with the "desperation" of the London riots. During the week of the October 2011 low in the S&P, I shared this thought in real time with my clients under the title "It's Around Here Somewhere":

> I'm going to go out on a limb to suggest that there is a bottom nearby. Whether that bottom happened near 1070 on the S&P on Tuesday or will happen shortly at a level below—or even well below—that level, we'll see; but to these eyes there are reflections of self-assured uncertainty everywhere I look.

---

[1] *Chronicle of the 20th Century* (Mount Kisco, NY: Chronicle Publications, 1987), 409.

This past week Forbes *ran a column by British historian Paul Johnson entitled "Who Can Lead Us To Safety;" while last Saturday Joe Queenan's column in* The Wall Street Journal *was headlined "Who's Our Daniel Boone or Joan of Arc?" And even* The Economist *jumped on the "rudderless" bandwagon with its cover recommending "Until politicians actually do something about the world economy...BE AFRAID."*

Then there were these comments from Moody's on Wednesday:

'There has been a profound loss of confidence in certain European sovereign debt markets, and Moody's considers that this extremely weak market sentiment will likely persist...It is no longer a temporary problem that might be addressed through liquidity support, and several euro-area governments are increasingly affected by the loss of confidence.'

Put simply, certainty has been lost and is not coming back any time soon; and we see no one who can rescue us from the deep end of the pool. Be afraid. Or at least that is what we now think.

The problem I have with all of this is that both tops and bottoms are defined by saturation. And of late, everyone from media pundits to parents on the sidelines at soccer games are talking about it. Europe has fallen and can't get up and we all now know it."[2]

Hopefully these examples have provided you with a sense of not only the financial decisions made at the bottom of a market, but also the political and social actions as well. In my own note to my clients, though, you saw that I was not at

---

[2] Peter W. Atwater, Financial Insyghts Commentary, October 7, 2011, 1. www.financial-insyghts.com/oct11_2011.html

all specific as to the price at which I thought the market bottomed. From my perspective there is a world of difference between sensing that from a social mood standpoint a bottom is near and proclaiming the price at which the bottom will occur. For what it's worth, the same can be said about market peaks as well.

I raise this point because many investors try to time bottoms and tops only to find that they have acted too soon, selling before a peak, for example, or purchasing before a bottom. Given that specific stocks, and markets in general, are subject to both "melt-ups" of self-assured certainty in which prices might rise dramatically at the very end of cycle and "melt-downs" of self-assured uncertainty in which prices do the reverse, to me the real value in understanding the social mood elements of tops and bottoms is that it enables you to prepare. To be able to say to yourself, "It's around here somewhere."

Most investors forget that there are 100 yards between the end zones of a significant trough and a significant peak in price and from an investing perspective you can still win the game starting on the 20-yard line on one end of the field and ending on the 20-yard line on the other end. By knowing when a market bottom is occurring it is much, much easier to wait for the turn to happen and then invest *after* the turn.

Social Mood and Invention

Before I discuss the current market, I want to make sure you don't come away with the thought that there are only negative aspects to the element of "sacrifice" that's found at the bottoms of social mood.

Beginning in mid-2009 I noticed a series of billboards with the tagline "Recession 101," which were intended to provide inspiration in the face of the steep market drop and economic decline the U.S. had experienced over the prior two years.

One of the Recession 101 signs I saw offered this thought: "Bill Gates started Microsoft in a recession." I highlight this line because another way to think of sacrifice is invention, or, more likely in Mr. Gates's case, personal re-invention. Although I will leave the coincidence of Microsoft's founding and an economic recession to others, I suspect that Mr. Gates (and Microsoft co-founder Paul Allen) were both operating with a very "me, here, now" mindset.

We don't say "Necessity is the mother of invention" for nothing.

But consider how the entire business cycle fits with the Horizon Preference framework and how rising confidence naturally moves an organization from the "me, here, now" beginning phase of invention through innovation and expansion and all the way to the "us, everywhere, forever" point of saturation and overreaching (see Figure 6.3).

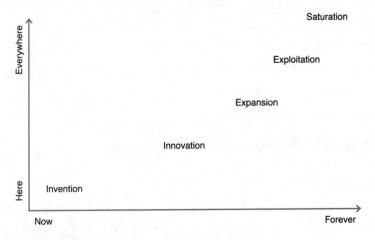

Figure 6.3 Horizon Preference and the business cycle

Source: Financial Insyghts

This is not to suggest that success is at all guaranteed. Most business leaders believe that their primary focus is sales and getting more products sold. I'd offer that leaders would be much better served by focusing on ways to boost confidence by others in their business. The upward-right migration in the business cycle requires greater and greater confidence to be shared by a larger and larger group of people—be they management, clients, investors, suppliers, lenders, and so on. That goes well beyond merely selling more. After watching the recent experience in the housing and banking sectors, leaders would be wise to consider where they are most vulnerable to deteriorating confidence.

The Contrast Between Eastman Kodak and Milliken & Co.

As I was writing this book, Eastman Kodak filed for bankruptcy after more than 100 years in business. One of the things that struck me in the many articles written around the time of the bankruptcy filing was how Kodak had invented the digital camera in 1975, but because the margins on film were so great, and it had a near-monopoly on film and cameras at the time, it was very slow to act and innovate with the new technology.

What is remarkable to me is how clearly one can see both the trend in confidence at Kodak as its near-monopoly in photography took hold during the 1960s and early 1970s and the malaise thereafter in the company's stock price (see Figure 6.4). Although the stock briefly rose above its 1973 peak just prior to the 1987 crash, it took almost 24 years before the company's stock reached an all-time high. But note that by that point, the company was already dismantling itself. In 1993, Eastman Chemical was spun off.

Eastman Kodak Company Common St

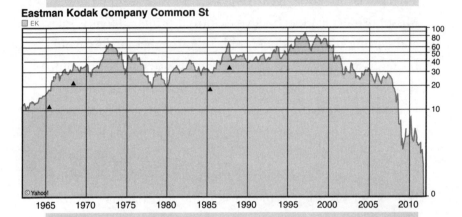

Figure 6.4 Eastman Kodak common stock performance from 1962 to 2012

Source: Yahoo! (chart)/CSI (data). Reproduced with permission of Yahoo! Inc.
© 2012 Yahoo! Inc. YAHOO! and the YAHOO! logo are registered trademarks of
Yahoo! Inc.

As I noted in Chapter 2, divestitures reflect deteriorating mood (and often management frustration), not
growing confidence. Few managers voluntarily sell their
winners.

I am sure that back in 1975 Kodak management didn't
think about it this way, but to me Kodak's unwillingness
to innovate and risk its high margin film business feels
an awful lot like "hoarding" and a desire to hold on to a
past believed to be more certain, because, particularly
in Kodak's case, that past was full of exceptional profits. By exhibiting this kind of hoarding behavior, I think
that Kodak was already in a state of decline; it just didn't
realize it.

What I also found interesting at the time of the Kodak
bankruptcy filing was a story in *The Wall Street Journal*
contrasting Kodak's demise to a far more positive experience of another long-standing American corporation, the

textile firm Milliken & Co., which also faced global competition and threats from innovation.[3] Where Kodak had resisted innovation, Milliken embraced it, thanks in large part to the culture established by Roger Milliken who, per the *Journal*, "pounded the drum for new products, new ideas and better manufacturing techniques—vision from the top that's evident at other innovative companies, both public and private."

I had the great fortune to meet Mr. Milliken near the end of his life and was struck by his thirst for knowledge and innovation wherever it might be found. I loved the fact that at more than 90 years of age he was, as his family put it, "still planting acorns." (And to that point, I thought it was completely fitting and in character that in 1963, Milliken & Co. converted much of its 650-acre corporate headquarters site into what is today the Milliken Arboretum containing one of the greatest tree collections in our country.)

I share this because as corporations grow and prosper many forget to keep planting acorns and instead try to hold on to their successes of the past, continuing to believe with self-assured certainty what the future will hold. For most corporations, the result is that their highest margin products become paralyzing, particularly as few have the courage to use the profits to foster invention and to fuel innovation, let alone try to sell the operation at the top. Instead they use the business to cover shortfalls elsewhere and to meet short-term business goals. They forget that they are in the confidence growing business.

---

[3] John Bussey, "The Anti-Kodak: How a U.S. Firm Innovates and Thrives," *The Wall Street Journal*, http://online.wsj.com/article/SB1 0001424052970203721704577157001419477034.html.

Final Thoughts

The deterioration in confidence that accompanies a decline in mood brings with it an increasing view of an uncertain future. The result is that we hoard with greater and greater intensity as mood falls. At the very bottom, though, when even hoarding no longer stems the mounting uncertainty, we experience self-assured uncertainty, and with it a visceral need to do something—sometimes literally anything—to make it stop.

What I have witnessed, though, in the actions exhibited at the bottom of mood, whether for an individual stock or for the market as a whole, is consistently some form of sacrifice—an act, no longer intended to preserve the past, but to change the future. And with it comes a widening Horizon Preference.

Much like major market peaks are accompanied by major expressions of permanence and generosity, major bottoms are marked by extreme hoarding/self-interest and, ultimately, sacrifice.

Having discussed the principles of Horizon Preference and how social mood affects our decision making and the markets in concept, I would like to take one very brief detour into the world of accounting before I turn to our current market and what I see today and what it suggests for the future.

Hopefully, you'll never look at earnings the same way ever again.

7

Cooking the Books: Corporate Earnings and Social Mood

For most investors, quarterly earnings are like a dinner at a restaurant. They either like the food or they don't. Even more importantly, although they may want to meet the chef, few diners ever really want to go into the kitchen to see how the food was prepared, and almost none want to be dragged through the recipe step by step, let alone taken to the slaughterhouse to see how farm-to-table dining really works.

The earnings rule is simple: Just put it on the plate. Don't make me understand how it got there.

To compensate for this general lack of interest and ability on the part of investors in understanding how earnings are actually arrived at, corporations have adopted any number of "alternative" presentations which, depending on the moment and the industry, ask investors to consider "non-GAAP" operating earnings that exclude what management believes to be either irrelevant or extraordinary elements, typically negative, in an effort to focus investors on what management believes to be "normal."

To go back to my restaurant analogy, it's like a waiter saying, "Besides the chicken we accidentally burnt and the broccoli that we know you don't like, your dinner was just like we always make it and the way you always like it—and, more importantly, how you should expect it the next time you are in."

I would note, however, that investors' willingness to overlook "burnt" earnings is directly tied to mood. During a bull market for a stock, investors ignore bad news believing it to be an anomaly—the chef is having a bad day. Conversely, during periods of falling mood, we extrapolate burnt earnings into the future, and as investors we look for a different place to eat. In bear markets, bad earnings news is financial food poisoning.

Mood-Driven Accounting Principles

Earnings presentation and our willingness or unwillingness to eat what has been served up by management, however, are merely the end of the earnings-preparation process. What few investors ever really consider is how much mood also affects both the recipes followed—established accounting principles—and the attitude of the chef—which specific recipe to use and just how much discretionary sugar or spice should go into revenues, expenses, assets, and liabilities during the quarter.

From my perspective, too many investors think of the accounting standards that govern financial statements as tablets inscribed by Moses—a set of irrevocable laws that have existed since the beginning of time. What these investors miss is that rather than predestined laws, financial accounting standards are nothing more than regulations that were established, like all other regulations, in response to changes in mood. The result is that we deregulate accounting all the way up a bull market and we re-regulate all the way down.

The consequence is that it is much easier for a corporation to generate $1.00 of earnings at the top of the market than it is at the bottom of the market.

As a pioneer in the non-mortgage securitization world, I had a front-row seat, sometimes literally, for observing the deregulation of the rules for when an asset such as a car or credit card loan could be treated as sold (and therefore taken off the balance sheet, often at a gain) by a bank or finance company and when it could not. What started as a clear focus on contract law at the start of my career evolved into rules focused on whether the "underlying risk of loss" (as determined by the management of the seller and signed off by the seller's auditors) associated with assets had been transferred to someone else.

Needless to say I was not at all surprised when in 2009, in the aftermath of the banking crisis, the Financial Accounting Standards Board (FASB) announced new rules for securitization accounting that forced the reconsolidation of more than $600 billion in credit card loan assets that had been previously considered to be sold and therefore off-balance sheet. The downturn in mood, particularly in the financial services industry, resulted in stricter rules.

But it was not just securitization accounting that benefitted from deregulation during the past 20 years. A quick look at the evolution of the accounting principles for acquisitions, derivatives, and other complex transactions from 1980 to the early 2000s all reflect the clear characteristics of loosening standards that naturally accompany bull markets and rising mood. (Not surprisingly, too, there was also an enormous industry-wide effort during this same period to create consistent global accounting standards as well, with teams from the FASB and the International Accounting Standards

Board (IASB) all working to establish one set of consistent rules for consolidated financial statements worldwide. Like other industries, the accounting world also embraced and reflected the "us, everywhere, forever" elements of peak social mood.)

Deregulation/reregulation of accounting rules, however, is only part of the story. Unbeknownst to most investors, accounting principles themselves frequently give companies choices as to how to book a specific asset or liability. For example, in banking a security may be accounted for using *mark-to-market* accounting or *held-to-maturity* accrual accounting. (It all depends on how long management intends to hold the instrument. But the distinction alters how and when gains and losses can or must be taken [as well as who determines the gain or loss] and how much capital a bank must hold against the asset.) During the period from 1990 to 2007, financial institutions loaded up on mark-to-market securities. I will spare the gory details, but suffice it to say that a company would not voluntarily opt for mark-to-market accounting if they saw the prospect for lower securities' values.

To me, both the regulators and investors missed the message of extreme management confidence implicit in the growth of mark-to-market assets on bank balance sheets. (For what it's worth, I'd also note that they also missed the extreme lack of management confidence as mark-to-market assets were "recharacterized" to held-to-maturity in enormous volume during late 2008 and early 2009 just as the markets were bottoming.)

What accounting rules corporations choose or don't choose reflects management confidence.

Mood-Driven Management Judgment

The third element I believe investors miss is how the specific chosen accounting rules are then applied by the companies and financial institutions who report earnings. In this regard, I believe most investors woefully under-appreciate the amount of management judgment that goes into the preparation of financial statements and how much that judgment is influenced by changes in mood.

In 2009, when the FASB adopted more conservative accounting rules for securitizations, Robert Herz, then chairman of the FASB, said the following in a press release:

> *[The] changes were proposed and considered to improve existing standards and to address concerns about companies who were stretching the use of off-balance sheet entities to the detriment of investors. The new standards eliminate existing exceptions, strengthen the standards relating to securitizations and special-purpose entities, and enhance disclosure requirements. They'll provide better transparency for investors about a company's activities and risks in these areas.*[1]

Companies had "stretched" and taken advantage of "existing exceptions" while limiting disclosure. Of course they had; even more so, thanks to rising mood, investors didn't care.

I'd note, however, that it is not just in complex accounting rules like securitization where management judgment comes into play. As a simple example, let's look at loan loss provisions,

---

[1] Financial Accounting Standards Board, "FASB Issues Statements 166 and 167 Pertaining to Securitizations and Special Purpose Entities," June 12, 2009, www.fasb.org/cs/ContentServer?c=FASBContent_C&pagename=FASB/FASBContent_C/NewsPage&cid=1176156240834.

and the amount a bank might need to set aside for potential credit losses in the future. The strong economic times that go along with rising mood naturally bring with them lower and lower levels of loss in loan portfolios (because more people are employed, earnings are rising, and so on) at the same time lenders become more and more confident and lend to weaker and weaker borrowers. (It is why, as I've stated before, loans default from the peak backward. The worst loan is always made at the top.)

But consider at the top how low credit loss percentages are thanks to both growing loan portfolios and declining losses; it is a proverbial buy-one-get-one-free as both denominator and numerator work in a bank's favor. In addition, if bank management is eagerly lending to weaker and weaker borrowers, there are no worries about future losses. At a peak in social mood, neither management nor their accountants (nor banking regulators, for that matter) see a need for higher loan loss provisions.

The loan loss provision on a bank balance sheet is just one example. There are literally hundreds of asset categories that rely on management judgment, including goodwill, net pension assets, deferred taxes, and so on. The same is true for liabilities. When and for how much a company reserves, say for litigation risk, is almost entirely dependent on management judgment.

In bull markets with their rising mood, the net result is that you have increasingly optimistic managers applying increasingly optimistic accounting rules while generating higher and higher levels of earnings that get less and less scrutiny and higher multiples by investors. (And people wonder how companies were reporting record earnings and profit margins!)

But appreciate the other side of the peak in mood. In bear markets, investors more closely scrutinize lower earnings, which are determined more conservatively by management applying more conservative accounting rules. At the same time, thanks to lower mood, investors then value those more conservatively prepared earnings less, resulting in lower P/E multiples as well.

And I am just scratching the surface. More conservative accounting is only one of the regulatory effects that comes with falling mood. Today, for example, the banking industry is not only more conservatively applying more conservative accounting policies (which are getting greater scrutiny), but the banks are also facing tighter operating regulations as well. From Dodd-Frank and the Durbin Amendment to Basel III, the industry is facing an onslaught of new rules. Suffice it to say that what would have been reported as a dollar's worth of earnings by the financial services industry three years ago is probably only 50 or 75 cents today.

I should add, though, that years from now, as social mood improves, substantially all the counter-cyclical risk-related rules and regulations being imposed on the banks today are almost certain to be lifted. The Glass-Steagall Act, which was passed in the aftermath of the 1929 stock market crash, was repealed by the Gramm-Leach-Bliley Act in 1999, just as social mood in the United States was peaking.

The rising tide of social mood lifts all rules, and that is why it is far easier to earn $1.00 worth of profit in periods of rising mood than in periods of falling mood.

Scrutiny and Social Mood

Over the past five years I have repeatedly told my clients to "never underestimate the inverse correlation between scrutiny and social mood." In good times, investors don't ask, and managers don't tell. In bad times, investors ask more probing questions and demand greater detail.

Nowhere has that been more evident recently than in the growing page counts of financial service firm 10-K's (annual reports filed with the SEC) since 2007. Despite in many cases a contraction in both scope and size, the major banks have been required to disclose more detailed information about their mortgage holdings, their European debt exposures, and so on.

It is probably too soon to determine whether it will be statistically significant, but I can't help but wonder whether the bottom of this financial crisis will be marked by a peaking in the average 10-K page count.

It is not just in regulatory filings, though, where the inverse correlation of mood and scrutiny comes into play. In late October 2011, in the aftermath of the MF Global collapse, the stock of Jefferies Group, a major investment bank, fell by 20% in just over an hour when investors became concerned about the company's exposure to European sovereign debt.

Shortly thereafter, the Heard on the Street column in *The Wall Street Journal* asked, "Is any amount of disclosure enough when it comes to a financial firm's exposure to Europe?"

And the column continued:

"As long as the doubts persist, big bank stocks can expect to be whipsawed by worries about Europe and financial contagion. A possible antidote is better disclosure about counterparty concentrations. Big banks aren't likely to do this on their own for fear peers won't follow suit. So it's time the Securities and Exchange Commission stepped in, calling for disclosures on counterparty concentrations and standardized information about country risks...

Granted, banks would likely balk at providing detail on even high-level counterparty exposure. For one, they may fear this additional information could highlight how much risk rests in a small group of about a dozen or so big, global banks. And they will be quick to point out that the additional information they've so far provided has hardly helped reassure investors.

But in this case, the perfect shouldn't be the enemy of the good. Better for big banks and the SEC to get ahead of the issue. Otherwise, like Jefferies, they risk being strip-searched at gunpoint by markets."[2]

Such is the power of a sudden decline in confidence. Not only do investors want to know more, they want to know it faster, too. It is "me, here, now." From my perspective, corporate executives would be wise to appreciate that falling share prices will be accompanied by greater demands for more detailed information. Too many executives believe that the market is being unreasonable. What they forget is that when one of their own business units is struggling,

---

[2] David Reilly, "Investors Can't See Banks for the Hedges," *The Wall Street Journal*, November 7, 2011, http://online.wsj.com/article/SB10001424052970204621904577018321991559232.html.

they too increase their own demands for more information. It is a natural outgrowth of deteriorating mood.

Finally, as I was completing this book in spring 2012, the headlines were filled with one accusation after another of alleged unsavory activities by the CEO of Chesapeake Energy. One look at the company's stock chart and the collapse of its common share price (as well as the price of the company's principal asset—natural gas), and the timing of those allegations is clear. All the excesses that are overlooked at the top get fully exposed at the bottom.

Needless to say, given the deterioration in mood (and not just at Chesapeake, but in general), I would not be at all surprised to see significant changes in both accounting and corporate governance regulations in the aftermath of this unfolding scandal. Much like Sarbanes-Oxley followed the collapse of Enron and WorldCom, there are likely to be new rules in the wake of Chesapeake.

On the flip side, though, the Chesapeake Energy scandal suggested to me a reason to be very optimistic about the future direction of natural gas prices in the spring of 2012—particularly as the troubles at Chesapeake were also accompanied by story after story about fracking and the process's ability to create an almost unlimited supply of natural gas for years to come.

Mood-Driven "One Time" Charges

There are other elements of mood-related accounting that I believe investors should also consider. It is always interesting to me to see what "one-time" write-downs a new CEO or CFO takes in the quarter after assuming office, particularly when the executive comes in from the outside. When these charges happen, they almost always reflect a change in mood and typically a more cautious outlook by the incoming executive. (And as an aside, I have always been surprised that boards of directors don't include compensation clawbacks for departing executives, as subsequent asset write-downs almost always relate to profits booked in prior periods.)

Changes in management are not the only time, though, when you can see corporate mood changes reflected in company accounting in real time.

In January 2012, as I was writing this book, *The Wall Street Journal* covered the fourth quarter 2011 earnings results from Ford and Procter & Gamble (P&G) on the same page.[3] In the Ford results, the *Journal* highlighted how the company had written up its deferred tax asset. (For those unfamiliar with what deferred tax assets are, they arise when a company takes a loss and books a tax credit that it expects to be able to benefit from later on.) In Ford's case, the company had written down its deferred tax asset when future earnings prospects (and the ability to use the tax benefit) were in serious doubt in 2006. By writing up the deferred tax asset, Ford was all but proclaiming substantially greater confidence in its future.

At P&G it was a completely different story. In its fourth quarter earnings, the company wrote off $1.5 billion in goodwill associated with the company's $7 billion acquisition of Wella in 2003 and its $57 billion purchase of Gillette in 2005. By its write downs, what P&G was proclaiming was that the cost of those acquisitions was too high and that the future earnings prospects from those divisions were no longer what

---

[3] Jeff Bennett, "Ford Cruises, but Woes Loom," and Paul Ziobro, "P&G Profit Slumps 49%," *The Wall Street Journal*, January 28-29, 2012, B3.

P&G had thought they would be when the companies were acquired.

To me, any time a company writes down the value of goodwill or deferred taxes or any other assets that relate to future earnings and revenues, investors should be asking management what that means in terms of revisions to management's earnings projections. At the same time, investors should hardly take consolation that these write downs are almost always portrayed by managers as "non-cash." To me, that is like an investor saying that the loss taken today on a bad stock investment purchased yesterday is non-cash. The only reason that these charges are non-cash is that the cash left the corporation in a prior period in an acquisition price that turned out to be too high. By tolerating non-cash charges, boards of directors and investors send managers a message that it is fine to overpay for acquisitions.

To be fair, though, it wasn't just boards and investors who sent that message to management. Over the past 25 years, there has been a significant deregulation of the accounting for acquisitions; and, as part of that, amortization of goodwill (the expensing of premiums related to acquisitions) was eliminated by the FASB. For corporations, there were clear earnings incentives to buy rather than build. And given the high level of social mood, neither management nor investors believed firms were overpaying.

Looking ahead, given the amount of goodwill that is now being written off by corporations relating to acquisitions done at the peak of the market (2005–2007), I would not be surprised to see more conservative accounting policies for mergers and acquisitions.

Needless to say, those new rules would not be earnings positive.

Final Thoughts

At its core, GAAP accounting is a regulation and is subject to the same mood-based influences seen elsewhere, such as in banking and nuclear energy. When we are confident, we deregulate. When we are uncertain, we reregulate. Even more, as both assets and liabilities reflect corporate management's mood, in periods of rising mood there is a natural exponential effect in which asset values are inflated and liabilities reduced by the increasingly optimistic application by management of increasingly lax accounting rules. During periods of deteriorating mood, the reverse is also true.

Although most investors find the tedium of accounting to be brain numbing, changes in both accounting rules and the application of those rules are clear indicators of the direction of social mood both at an individual corporate level and for the markets as a whole. That said, accounting policy changes, like all regulations, will almost certainly follow the change in mood. The Committee on Accounting Procedure (CAP), the first private sector organization that had the task of setting accounting standards in the United States, for example, did not come into being until 1936, well after the market bottom. The FASB was formed in 1973, near the end of the late 1960s/early 1970s bear market, and the Public Company Accounting Oversight Board (PCAOB) was established in 2002 with the passage of Sarbanes-Oxley after the failure of Enron and WorldCom. All followed, rather than led, events.

One final point related to the correlation of earnings and social mood. As I was finishing up this book, *The Wall Street Journal* noted that over the past 10 years fewer and fewer companies have been providing quarterly or annual earnings guidance.[4] Looking at the deterioration in social mood over that same period, that news is hardly surprising. With lower confidence, companies are less willing to commit to what they think will happen in the future, particularly, as I noted earlier, as falling mood brings tighter accounting rules and more conservative application of those tighter rules.

I think it is safe to say that when social mood improves we will see a rise in companies offering earnings guidance as well.

I realize that this has been a lengthy detour into a topic that most investors would much rather avoid, but the direction of social mood plays a much more significant role in how corporate earnings are arrived at than people think. To go back to my dinner analogy at the top of this chapter, changes in mood not only affect what goes on the plate and how much we like it, but the portion size and how the meal was prepared as well. The entire earnings process is mood affected.

Next I turn to where I see the markets today. Hopefully this chapter has helped set the stage. By better understanding how mood affects the earnings process—and more importantly how changes in mood are already affecting that process—I believe investors will be much better prepared for what is ahead.

---

[4] Baruch Lev, "The Case for Guidance," *The Wall Street Journal*, February 27, 2012, R3.

8

Social Mood and the Markets Today: So Where Are We?

To frame my answer to the question in the chapter's title, I'd like to begin by asking two questions, which I frequently use to launch my presentations on Horizon Preference. The first question is, "We know things aren't as good as they used to be, so when were they the best?" And the second question is, "As bad as things are today, is there a time you can think of when things were far worse?"

Before reading on, I encourage you to think about your answers to both of these questions and, if possible, to put specific dates on them.

When I am speaking to groups, after giving everyone the opportunity to silently answer the two questions I just raised, I typically call on members of the audience to give their answers. What is remarkable to me is how, with no prompting, groups quickly and consistently arrive at a collective answer to each question.

To start in reverse, the answer to the second question is universally "the bottom of the Great Depression." And although few can put a specific date on it when asked, they all *know* that the Great Depression was *the* bottom. At least in modern times, in the minds of most Americans, things have never been worse.

Interestingly, though, the answer to the first question generates two very different clusters of dates. For *the* top, a broad, diverse audience always seems to settle somewhere in the late 1990s and early 2000s—with the most frequent comment being "before 9/11" (with one person in an audience even putting a very specific date of September 10, 2001 on it). When I speak to executives in multinational corporations or in financial services, however, they choose later dates: "2006/2007" or "before the banking crisis" being the most popular.

Seeing why a broad group of individuals would think that the late 1990s and early 2000s represented the top, is easy when you look at a chart like Figure 8.1, which plots the S&P 500 against the Bloomberg Consumer Comfort Index.

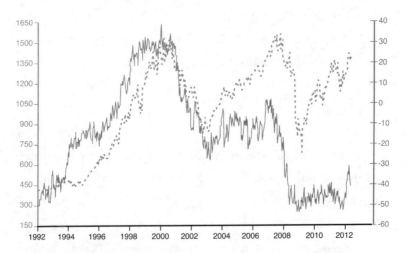

Figure 8.1 The Bloomberg Consumer Comfort Index versus the S&P 500 (in nominal terms), 1992–2012

Source: MacroMavens

Without question, mood, at least as measured by the Bloomberg Consumer Comfort Index, topped in 2000. But note how the S&P 500 went on to peak in 2007 whereas the Consumer Comfort Index bounced from its early 2003 low to a lower high. As the KBW Banking Index (what I consider to be a very good proxy for the mood of the financial services industry) also went on to reach a record higher high in 2007, I believe the chart in Figure 8.1 helps to explain why multinational executives and financial services professionals choose a later date than most Americans. For them, their mood did peak later.

I can imagine some readers have gone back to the beginning of the book and are asking themselves "What did I miss? I thought mood and broad market indices were supposed to track closely!" Needless to say, I too struggled mightily with that question. For several months I had a difficult time trying to bridge the gap between what the major consumer confidence indices were reporting and what I saw in the S&P 500 and the Dow.

Then Stephanie Pomboy of MacroMavens shared the chart in Figure 8.2 with me.

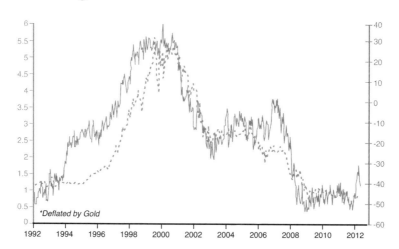

Figure 8.2 The Bloomberg Consumer Comfort Index versus the S&P 500 (divided by the price of gold), 1992–2012

Source: MacroMavens

What is different about this second chart from the first one is that, rather than presenting the S&P 500 in nominal terms, it presents the index deflated by the price of gold. That is to say, that measured in real terms, mood and the markets overlap nearly perfectly.

I hope that someday those responsible for monetary policy in our country will study these charts because they suggest that although the Federal Reserve can lift nominal asset values through currency devaluation, there is little the Federal Reserve and other monetary policymakers can do to affect mood.

Hopefully, though, Figures 8.1 and 8.2 will help more than just a few readers understand why their own moods have felt uncomfortably disconnected from the normal rising confidence that they have experienced in the past during periods of rising stock prices. Nominal stock prices have moved higher thanks to the extreme actions of monetary policymakers whereas real stock prices have followed social mood lower.

As the chart in Figure 8.2 shows, since early 2000 social mood has been declining steadily. Even more importantly, since the stock market bottom in early 2009, while the broad markets have doubled in value, little of that has been felt by most Americans. In fact, whether measured by the market in real terms or by the Bloomberg Consumer Comfort Index, mood in early October 2011 was even lower than it was when the market bottomed in 2009. That is 12 years of deteriorating mood—nearly four times the length of the decline during the Great Depression.

Modern Day Extremes in Social Mood

As you can see from the charts in Figures 8.1 and 8.2, whether someone picks 2000 or 2007 as the peak, there is no difference measured in real terms. (For what it's worth, I believe that the reason executives reference a mood peak that aligns with the peak in the markets is because the moods of executives overall are much more "leveraged" than the average American to the nominal value of financial assets because a much greater amount of their own compensation and net worth is as well.)

But what is so important to me about an audience's ability to collectively pick both "the Great Depression" and "2000" is that without even realizing it and with little prompting, people can identify the two bookends to our social mood spectrum over the past 100 years. The bottom, filled with self-assured uncertainty, was the Great Depression whereas the top, filled with self-assured certainty, was somewhere during the past decade. Today we feel better than we did during the Great Depression, but worse than we did not too long ago.

Why these bookends are so important to me is that they enable me to overlay the Horizon Preference framework on a long-term chart of the Dow Jones Industrial Average (Figure 8.3) and to test its relevance and accuracy. Importantly, and to go back to the "characteristics" of rising mood presented in Chapter 2, "Horizon Preference: How Mood Affects Our Decision Making," it enables me to look at our behaviors over this very protracted timeline to see whether those behaviors became more and more extreme over the timeframe as social mood rose. Did we, for example, deregulate to greater and greater extremes as mood and the markets rose? Did companies become more global and so on? Were there greater levels of bipartisanship?

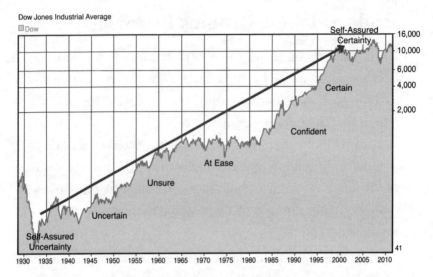

Figure 8.3 1933 to 2000: Self-assured uncertainty to self-assured certainty

Source: Yahoo! (chart)/CSI (data). Reproduced with permission of Yahoo! Inc. © 2012 Yahoo! Inc. YAHOO! and the YAHOO! logo are registered trademarks of Yahoo! Inc.

Admittedly, the rising line in mood is not straight. The late 1960s and early 1970s, for example, stands out as a period in which our behaviors suggest a significant downturn in social mood. Still, no one has yet suggested to me that that period reflected a lower bottoming of mood than the Great Depression.

What does stand out, however, is how consistently our positive mood-related behaviors show more extremes during the late 1990s than they did during the 1950s and 1960s. We borrowed more. We built bigger houses. There was greater peace in the world. If the post-Depression era was "less bad" and the post-war period of the 1950s and early 1960s was "good" if not "better," the late 1990s and early 2000s period was clearly "best." Or at least that is what we thought. More importantly, that is how we acted.

Although I am not saying that markets can't or won't rise over their 2000 or 2007 peaks, I think it is important to consider that in order for that to happen our underlying behaviors must reflect even greater extremes of confidence. Needless to say, I struggle with that thought—at least in the near term.

There are other aspects about the peak we experienced over the past decade that I think are also important in considering its significance.

Communication and Transportation Innovations and Peaks in Social Mood

As I pointed out in Chapter 3, "Market Peaks and All the Red Flags They Wave," the dot.com bubble offered an extraordinary window into "self-assured certainty." We all believed that the Internet changed our world forever everywhere, and we even valued concept stocks accordingly (or maybe it should be accordion-ingly, given how far valuations were stretched). There was an extraordinary extrapolation of the present into the future.

What is significant to me, though, is that this was not the first time that the extrapolation of innovative communication and transportation technology has accompanied a very major market peak. From canals in the 1830s to trains and Morse code in the late 1800s to automobiles and radio in the 1920s to air and space travel and television in the 1960s, major market peaks and major "socially interconnecting" and "world-changing" technologies align (see Figure 8.4). Given our strongly positive mood at peaks, we consistently eagerly embrace innovative and expansive technologies and see the potential for "permanent" change everywhere. And investors put extremely high values on those companies that we believe will deliver this new certain future as well.

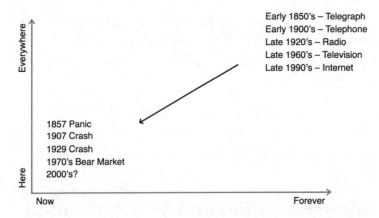

Figure 8.4 "Connectivity" innovations tie to significant market peaks
Source: Financial Insyghts

Please consider, though, the extraordinary "game-changing" nature of the Internet and its effect on all aspects of society—economically, politically, socially—on a global scale. I would not discount what this suggests as far as the extreme nature of our recent peak in social mood.

2000 to 2012: Deteriorating Mood

The peak characteristics that I see go well beyond the technology of the Internet. Just consider the distinction in how we saw the world in 2000 (see Figure 8.5) from how we see it today (see Figure 8.6) in 2012.

Permanence

Ownership

Replace

Multinational if not "Transnational"

Compromise

Middle Ground

Interconnected

Expansionism and Acquisitions

Just in Time Inventory

Concept Stocks

Figure 8.5 Characteristics of peak social mood
Source: Financial Insyghts

Transitory
Rent and Borrow
Repair
Local
Disagreement
Extremism
Independent
Protectionism and Divestitures
Just in Case Inventory
Dividend Stocks

Figure 8.6 Characteristics of weak social mood
Source: Financial Insyghts

Across all three Horizon Preference dimensions—time, distance, and relationships—it is as if our world has shrunk. Where we saw limitless opportunity in 2000, today we see considerably more uncertainty. (Again, though, I think it is important to appreciate that neither view is more or less correct or rational than the other. To go back to Figure 1.2, the world is no more or less certain today than it was in 2000. What has changed is our level of confidence. The change in our social mood has changed our perception of certainty.)

Social Mood and Public Policy Decisions

For policymakers, changes in our Horizon Preference create tailwinds and headwinds, depending on direction. Needless to say, over the past decade declining social mood has generated enormous headwinds to economic growth. Nowhere has that been clearer than in housing, where, despite record low mortgage rates and record affordability, Americans want to rent, rather than own, homes.

It was very interesting to me to see policymakers at the Federal Reserve explicitly admit their consternation as it relates to the mood-related change in consumer housing behavior earlier this year. In a speech in January 2012, for example, Federal Reserve governor Elizabeth Duke offered:

> *The Federal Reserve has already acted to reduce mortgage rates by purchasing longer-term assets, in particular through the purchase of agency mortgage-backed securities. Indeed, low rates combined with falling house prices have contributed to historically high levels of housing affordability. At the same time, rents have been rising, which should make home-ownership a more attractive option relative to rental housing.*
>
> *Despite this record affordability, home purchase and mortgage refinancing activity remains muted. The failure of home sales to respond to conditions that would otherwise seem favorable to home purchases indicates that there are other factors weighing on demand for owner-occupied homes.[1]*

To me those "other factors" relate to social mood. To the Federal Reserve, though, consumers were behaving irrationally. Consumers were choosing to rent, notwithstanding rapidly rising rents, record-low mortgage rates, and record affordability.

From a Horizon Preference perspective, however, consumers were doing exactly what they should do. Given the deterioration in mood, they wanted to rent rather than own because with lower confidence (and our perception of

---

[1] Elizabeth A. Duke, "Economic Developments, Risks to the Outlook, and Housing Market Policies," Virginia Bankers Association/Virginia Chamber of Commerce 2012 Financial Forecast, Richmond, Virginia, January 6, 2012.

greater uncertainty) we naturally prefer temporary, rather than permanent, solutions.

Although it is not entirely clear to me that Federal Reserve officials fully understand why Americans want to rent, I have to say that I was delighted to see them at least acknowledge that there is little more at this point they can do to promote homeownership and instead are choosing to focus their efforts on ways to promote home rental solutions rather than home purchases.

Still, it feels to me like we are taking baby steps. At the bottom of the housing market (and no, I don't think we are there yet), I expect that policymakers will throw away "homeownership" altogether as a meaningful measure and focus instead on "home occupancy" in which both temporary and permanent solutions are equally embraced.

For those looking for entrepreneurial opportunities in housing, the world of single-family rental property management and maintenance looks very promising to me (as do other businesses which take advantage of both consumer and corporate preferences for all things "temporary" today).

Plotting Social Mood

Several years ago, before I had fully developed the Horizon Preference model I use today, I offered the chart in Figure 8.7 in a client presentation.

My goal with the chart was to help one of my clients appreciate the dramatic changes in behavior I had seen between the peak in mood in 2000 and the 2009 market low. Where

2000 was "us, everywhere, forever," the bottom of the banking crisis was unequivocally "me, here, now."

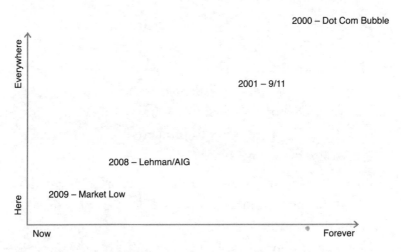

Figure 8.7 Our shrinking view of the world
Source: Financial Insyghts

In 2011, as I was "socializing" many of the concepts of this book, I had a conversation with Dave Allman at Elliott Wave International (EWI), and I offered the same chart on a conference call. After seeing the chart, Dave immediately asked me to stop my presentation while he emailed me a variation of this chart in Figure 8.8 that EWI had done for its clients.

In the same way that I had plotted specific years against the Horizon Preference framework, what EWI had done was to plot the same years using two significant valuation methods—price to book and bond yield to stock yield. Hopefully, thanks to this book, it is now easier to see how changes in confidence alter our Horizon Preference and, in turn, how we value stocks, and how and why these two charts tie together.

Credit: Robert R. Prechter, Jr., Elliott Wave International

Figure 8.8 Year-end stock market valuation 2000–2008

Now, let me offer the full version of the chart that Dave first offered me on our conference call (see Figure 8.9). Instead of just 2000 to 2008, (which are presented in Figure 8.8) what EWI had plotted was the entire period from 1927 to 2011.

As you can see from the EWI chart, every one of the past 20 years is in the upper-right quadrant of the chart, with 1999 and 2000, the real market peak and the peak social mood, at the very far upper right. I realize that for many readers the notion that what we have experienced over the past 20 years represents a severe valuation anomaly—even with the 2009 low—may be hard to swallow, but I would strongly encourage you to consider that possibility.

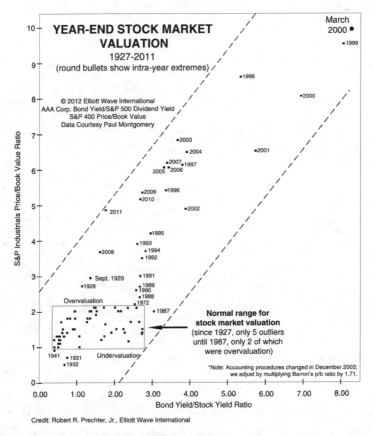

Credit: Robert R. Prechter, Jr., Elliott Wave International

Figure 8.9 Year-end stock market valuation 1927–2011

A Long-Term Perspective on Social Mood and Stock Multiples

During the late fall of 2011 as I was writing this book, I saw many analyst reports suggesting that stocks were cheap, with most using charts of price to earnings (P/E) multiples from 1990 to support their assertions. (P/Es in the fall of 2011 were roughly equal to those in 1990, the lowest point on many analysts' charts.) In fact, after reading several reports, I got the sense that to suggest that stock multiples could fall below 1990 was once again all but equivalent to believing that night doesn't follow day. In the world of investing, 20 years is a lifetime, and to suggest that a full market cycle is not captured in such a long timeframe suggests heresy.

But please consider the chart in Figure 8.10 from Jim Bianco of Bianco Research.

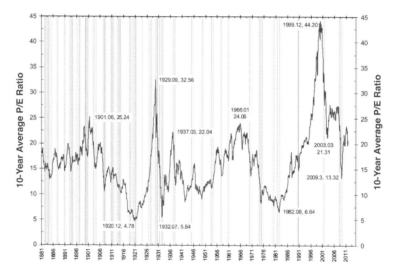

Figure 8.10 10-year average price/earnings ratio, 1981–2012
Source: Bianco Research

Sure, measured over the past 25 years equity valuations look cheap. Relative to the past 130 years, however, that is not true at all.

Here is where I think looking at the longer timeframe is so helpful. In 1937, when the mood was less bad than the Great Depression, stocks had a peak multiple of 22; then in 1966, when mood was "better" P/Es were 24; and in 2000 when mood was "great" P/Es were 44. Mood and P/E multiples tie.

But notice the P/E multiples at the significant lows on the chart. At the major bottoms (1920, 1932, 1982), P/Es fell to mid-single digits. Given that the stock multiple we experienced in 2000 was almost 1.4 times the peak P/E in 1929, I think investors must consider the real possibility that valuations could move to an opposite extreme with low single-digit P/E multiples before stocks begin another meaningful bull market.

Social Mood and the Evolution of Major Corporations

There is yet one other element to our 2000–2007 peak that gives me even greater pause. During the bear market of the late 1960s and early 1970s, with that period's deterioration in mood and "me, here, now" Horizon Preference, there was considerable public and political backlash to the perceived power wielded by multinational corporations, with a number of books from the period even suggesting that some multinational corporations (such as ITT) had usurped the rights and responsibilities historically associated with national governments.

Over the past 40 years, the "multinational" business model of American and European corporations doing business globally has morphed into "transnationalism" in which the world's largest corporations are truly global—in their management teams, their supply chains, their product distribution systems, and their shareholders. They are today to Main Street what the IMF is to town council—super-sovereign entities.

My concern is that the transnationalism of the world's largest corporations both reflects and represents an extraordinary peak in social mood—not just in the United States, but globally. In fact, from a Horizon Preference perspective, it is hard to see a business model that captures better the "us, everywhere, forever" elements of peak social mood than the extremes in business transnationalism I see today. At the world's largest corporations, the frictionless migration of labor, goods, capital, and data is considered a given, and not just for the production of simple items. Just look at the new Boeing 787 Dreamliner, for example, with its extraordinarily complex global sourcing, global assembly, global financing, and global client base. Talk about the presumption and extrapolation of "us, everywhere, forever."

For the shareholders of transnational corporations the benefits have been obvious over the past 20 years. One need only look at S&P 100 profit margin expansion over the period to see the quantification of those benefits (admittedly assisted by the mood-related accounting tailwind discussed in Chapter 7, "Cooking the Books: Corporate Earnings and Social Mood"). I am afraid, though, that transnational corporations are extraordinarily vulnerable to the nationalist backlash that naturally accompanies deteriorating social mood. Recently *The New York Times* offered a cover story titled, "How the U.S. Lost out on iPhone Work," which highlighted the cost and production benefits to Apple arising from Chinese manufacturing. But the article also offered this thought:

> *"Apple's an example of why it's so hard to create middle-class jobs in the U.S. now," said Jared Bernstein, who until last year was an economic adviser to the White House. "If it's the pinnacle of capitalism, we should be worried.*[2]

---

[2] Charles Duhigg and Keith Bradsher, "How the United States Lost Out on iPhone Work," *The New York Times*, January 22, 2012, 1.

And then there was this comment from the article as well:

"We sell iPhones in over a hundred countries," a current Apple executive said. "We don't have an obligation to solve America's problems. Our only obligation is making the best product possible."[3]

With deterioration in social mood likely to be accompanied by higher levels of unemployment, I worry that transnational corporations' seemingly sole allegiance to their global shareholders is likely to make them easy targets for the same political vilification we saw in 2009 toward Wall Street.

But there is yet another overlay for transnational corporations that suggests a far greater mood-related challenge than just these companies' ill-fitting supra-sovereign business model: the financial challenge currently facing most western sovereign nations today.

Not only are transnational corporations likely to be targets of hostile nationalistic political rhetoric like they were in the early 1970s, but I suspect that these companies' relative financial strength and non-native status will make them ripe for financial "burden sharing" along with other foreign creditors. (In that regard, note this line from a recent Reuter's story on European drug makers that "Cash-strapped governments have slashed drug prices [and] racked up close to $20 billion in unpaid bills for treatments....")[4]

Although I don't wish for it, it is not hard for me to see a scenario play out in which deteriorating social mood in Europe and the U.S. results in greater political and social pressure on transnational corporations, which significantly weakens profit

[3] Ibid.

[4] Ben Hirschler, "Analysis: Drugmakers relegate Europe as crisis saps returns," Reuters, February 15, 2012, www.reuters.com/article/2012/02/15/us-europe-pharmaceuticals-idustre81e15z20120215.

margins and P/E multiples. With weak economic growth, it is a zero-sum game, and I see few choices for policymakers other than to go after the biggest of big business.

Then, of course, there are the issues of national security, which also align with social mood. Deteriorating social mood, with its natural nationalism and heightened concerns about safety, are likely to drive demands for local sourcing, employment, and manufacturing of key national security supplies—without regard to what this may mean to corporate earnings. With western governments already stretched, I expect that calls for patriotic "sacrifice" will eat further into big corporation profit margins.

Weak Social Mood and Global Merger Backlash

To me one of the clearest examples to date of the challenges now faced by transnational corporations in a world of falling social mood and heightened nationalism has been in stock exchange M&A and the collapse of both the NYSE Euronext/Deutsche Boerse and the TMX (Toronto Stock Exchange)/London Stock Exchange mergers. Both deals drew intense regulatory scrutiny and the TMX/LSE deal even prompted an overtly nationalistic competing bid from a consortium aptly called the Maple Group made up of thirteen of Canada's largest financial institutions and pension funds.

Should mood deteriorate further, large cross-border M&A will be all but impossible to execute. Even domestic transactions will face greater challenges, particularly in industries already viewed by the public as either oligopolistic or overly complex. (In that regard it was no surprise to see the

Federal Reserve move very slowly on Capital One's recent acquisition of ING Direct.)

So long as mood is rising, few care about the move to larger, more globally complex business models. Falling mood, however, brings the reverse sentiment. With news series such as ABC's *Made in America* even profiling a family in Texas that emptied its home of everything but American-made products, it is not hard to see images that reflect and represent the clear shift in sentiment.

As I look at the world today, few large corporations appear to be concerned about, let alone prepared for, the kind of downside scenario further deterioration in social mood will bring. I suspect that, like most investors, business leaders see the past 20 years as indicative of the full potential range for what might be ahead.

Peak Social Mood and Sovereign Debt

Finally, to bring the discussion back to my original concern regarding sovereign debt, I can't help but wonder today whether there is also an unprecedented Big Truth now at risk.

In late 2010, the European fixed income team at Morgan Stanley offered this thought:

...the bonds of several peripheral countries, while still being government bonds in name, no longer offer the advantages of a government bond—safety, liquidity, low volatility and a negative correlation with risky assets.... Hence, investors running a traditional government portfolio are exiting those markets. In short,

*peripheral government bonds have become an asset
class in search of a new investor base.*[5]

Today, the idea that it is hard to find buyers for the sovereign debt of Europe's periphery nations hardly seems radical. The Big Truth of "safety, liquidity, low volatility and a negative correlation with risky assets" for those countries has been proved without question to now be false.

But note this observation from *The Wall Street Journal*'s Heard on the Street Column from February 23, 2012: "It used to be so simple. Developed-country government bonds were risk-free, while corporate bonds carried credit risk to varying degrees. The euro-zone crisis has exposed that assumption to be false."[6] Needless to say the bursting of a western government—and not just a European periphery—sovereign debt Big Truth has enormous implications for investors and governments alike.

Over the past 20 years major western governments were able to borrow record amounts at lower and lower interest rates thanks largely to an extreme peak in social mood. As we have already seen in Greece, however, falling social mood brings with it not just lower stock markets but also an unwillingness on the part of bond investors to lend to governments.

Further, for sovereign debt investors I think it is important to consider that whatever "firewalls" policymakers construct, the effectiveness of those firewalls is entirely based on social mood. As noted earlier, in October 2011 as mood was bottoming, no one believed that policymakers were either

---

[5] Joseph Cotterill, "If not the ECB, whom?," *Financial Times* (blog), December 2, 2010, http://ftalphaville.ft.com/blog/2010/12/02/425256/if-not-the-ecb-whom/.

[6] Richard Barley, "Bond Myths Are Exposed by Greece," *The Wall Street Journal*, February 23, 2012, C18.

willing or able to support the market. As mood then rose into the first quarter of 2012, however, the markets became more and more convinced (as did policymakers) that the incremental steps taken (all during rising social mood) would be sufficient to firewall the periphery.

I don't pretend to know where this leads at this point, but the idea that the euro-zone crisis has now exposed a very large Big Truth to be false—namely that developed-country government bonds are risk-free—worries me enormously. From Modern Portfolio Theory to issues of national and international security, to the collateral markets underpinning the global capital markets, I am afraid that the discrediting of the risk-free, developed-country sovereign debt Big Truth raises profound questions for all investors.

Still, the fact that so many investors globally believed and continue to believe this Big Truth, I am afraid, also speaks to the magnitude of this past decade's market peak.

Final Thoughts

To me, there are so many aspects of peak social mood that we experienced across business, technology, politics, and culture over the past decade that I think it is naïve to assume that the markets will move forward without a material market bottom that reflects a comparable extreme reflection of self-assured uncertainty. Yes, the March 2009 low was significant; unfortunately I am afraid it was not significant enough—either in its depth or its breadth. The 2000/2007 peak was more than just a market peak, it was a milestone in the broad representation of positive social mood. As I believe that mood moves in natural rhythmic cycles, I think readers need to contemplate, if not prepare for, a comparable mile-stone in negative social mood.

That said, markets do not move in a straight line either up or down. Even if I am ultimately correct in my view that the markets will hit single-digit P/Es before the next major bull market begins, there will be plenty of interim meaning-ful peaks and troughs along the way, which I hope this book helps you spot.

As I noted earlier, before I came to socionomics and developed the Horizon Preference framework, I learned the hard way what holding on to a long-term belief can do to investment returns in volatile markets such as the ones we have experienced over the past decade.

Today, while I maintain my long-term view, based on my belief that over the past decade what we experienced was a very significant peak in confidence and social mood, I instead watch closely for less significant peaks and valleys in the mar-ket so that I can take better advantage of meaningful market swings. In the next chapter, I share how.

9

Using Horizon Preference No Matter Your Long-Term View

As I offered in my introduction, my goal in writing this book is to share the insights and conclusions I have come to through the framework of socionomics. My hope is to help investors see what I now see in the markets and the world around us so that they can prosper from it. I was not trying to write either a Dow 50,000 or Dow 5,000 book.

To be clear, I hope my mood-based assessment of the past 20 years is not just wrong, but that it's very wrong. I don't wish for single digit P/Es nor the societal behavior that would naturally accompany a market defined by severe self-assured uncertainty. But it makes sense to me that confidence would follow a cyclical pattern (such as suggested in the chart in Figure 9.1) in which positive trends in mood naturally lead to a peak and overconfidence, which in turn lead to negative trends in mood that ultimately result in "under" confidence and a natural bottom, which would in turn lead to a positive trend in mood....

Given the significant peak in social mood we experienced between 2000 and 2007, I believe there is a significant trough in the future. Still, having looked at behaviors using the Horizon Preference framework and the principles of socionomics over long periods of time, I think it is important to appreciate that there are short-term cycles within long-term cycles, which are also significant and "tradable" for most investors, and which follow the same peak to trough to peak to trough patterns of confidence shown in Figure 9.1.

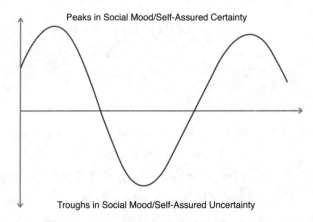

Peaks in Social Mood/Self-Assured Certainty

Troughs in Social Mood/Self-Assured Uncertainty

Figure 9.1 Social mood moves through a natural cycle

In Chapter 8, "Social Moods and the Markets Today: So Where Are We?," Figure 8.3 suggested that the entire period from the bottom of the Great Depression to 2000/2007 could be considered a move across the entire Horizon Preference framework from severe self-assured uncertainty to severe self-assured certainty. You could argue the same holds true, however, for the period from 1937 to 1966 or from 1990 to 2000. Both of those shorter time periods show similar behavioral swings from a trough to a peak in confidence just to a lesser degree. Even Figure 9.2 of the markets from the bottom in 2002 to the peak in 2007 suggests the same positive migration in mood, albeit to an even lesser degree.

Based on the work I have done looking at patterns of behavior, I believe that most investors should be able to routinely spot, using real-world events, significant market turning points using socionomics and the Horizon Preference framework presented in this book—turning points that suggest anywhere from a multi-month to multi-year change in market direction.

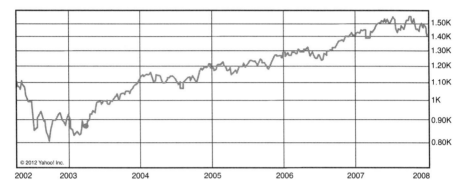

Figure 9.2 S&P 500 from 2002 to 2007

Source: Yahoo! (chart)/CSI (data). Reproduced with permission of Yahoo! Inc. © 2012 Yahoo! Inc. YAHOO! and the YAHOO! logo are registered trademarks of Yahoo! Inc.

As I discussed earlier, in early October 2011 I saw what I believed were consistent behaviors associated with self-assured uncertainty. Those behaviors suggested that a significant market bottom was near. Four months later, in early February 2012, I put together this lengthy list of behaviors that I saw at the time, which seemed to be reflecting just the opposite mood—an extremely high level of confidence, if not self-assured certainty—and what I believed was a highly likely peak in the market:

- *A $25 billion foreclosure settlement agreement among the major mortgage servicing banks, the state attorneys general, and HUD.*

- *The approval of a highly controversial "deal" on additional austerity in the Greek parliament.*

- *The announcement of a $90 billion merger deal by Glencore and Xstrata.*

- *The announcement by European Central Bank (ECB) President Mario Draghi that the ECB would expand the eligible collateral pool to loans and other financial assets, and Mr. Draghi's public statement, "Sure, it's going to be more risky. Does that mean that we take more risk? Yes, it means we take more risk. Does it mean this risk is being unmanaged? No, it is being managed. And it's being—it's going to be managed very well because really there will be a strong overcollateralization for the additional credit claims. The conditions will be very stringent." And Mr. Draghi's bullying comments to European bank CEOs, questioning the "virility" of those not participating in the long-term refinancing operation (LTRO).*

- *The thunderous initial public offering (IPO) announcement of Facebook and the IPO of Caesars Entertainment with the near-doubling of that company's stock price on the first day of trading.*

- *The meeting between President Obama and Italian Prime Minister Monti, accompanied by headlines touting "spectacular progress."*

- *News reports that the Council of Economic Advisers had "updated their forecasts in recent days and now project that the economy will create two million jobs this year if stimulus measures are extended, which could reduce the unemployment rate to about 8% by year's end."*

- *The parabolic move in Apple stock, with the world's largest stock (by market cap) rising more than 10% in four days, with TV pundits suggesting that investors now use call options to gain exposure to the stock because "1,000 shares are the price of a house."*

- *The lowest jobless claims since April 2008.*

- *The approval by the Nuclear Regulatory Commission of the first new nuclear reactor since 1978.*

- *Reductions in most commodity collateral margin requirements by the Chicago Mercantile Exchange.*

- *Passage of an insider trading law by and for Congress.*

- *German chancellor Angela Merkel's highest approval ratings since 2009.*

- *The eviction of the last Occupy Washington participants.*

- *The most successful meth drug raid ever in Mexico, capturing "an amount equal to half of all the meth seized worldwide in 2009," and the largest mass drug arrest in Colorado history involving 500 officers, 80 suspects, and 4 cocaine drug rings.*

- *Comments like this one from Neelie Kroes, a Dutch vice-president of the European Commission who told the Volkskrant newspaper, "It is absolutely not a case of man overboard if someone leaves the eurozone. It's always said: if you let one nation go, or ask one to leave, the entire structure will collapse. But that is just not true...."*

- *The denouncement of bonds by several major money managers, with one even suggesting that investors should have "100% in equities."*

- *An article from* The Wall Street Journal *entitled "Living Extra Large" about mega-mansions, with the accompanying sub-headline "When 50,000 Square Feet Isn't Enough."*[1]

A pretty striking contrast in behaviors in just four months, if you ask me!

---

[1] Peter Atwater, Financial Insyghts "Commentary," February 10, 2012, 2-3.

But the markets also reflected the change in mood as well with the S&P 500 rising more than 25% from early October 2011 to early February 2012.

Admittedly, I was early with my February observations. After pausing until early March, the markets continued higher over the next six weeks, gaining another 5%. (Although I want to note that many major European markets peaked in early February, as did the Dow Transports). As highlighted earlier in the book, confidence has a way of routinely morphing into over-confidence with "blow off" tops during which bad news is routinely ignored and self-assured certainty fills the airwaves. At the top, we don't want certainty to end. During March, this became clear as market participants renamed CNBC and Bloomberg Television "Apple TV." It was all the pundits wanted to talk about, and not surprisingly Apple stock, which had risen 22% in February, soared an additional 13% in March.

Still, in retrospect, the indicators of self-assured certainty that I saw and shared in early February were significant. While I didn't know it at the time, the peak in Apple's relative strength index (RSI) occurred that week and as Figure 9.3 shows, that week also marked a significant peak for the percentage of NYSE stocks trading above their 50-day moving average.

What socionomics and the Horizon Preference framework gave me in February was the ability to use real world indicators to see—without even realizing it—what was happening technically in the market. Confidence was peaking. And knowing that peaks are a process, given our natural optimism and desire to hold on to certainty for as long as we can, I could then be watchful for an upcoming change in the market's direction.

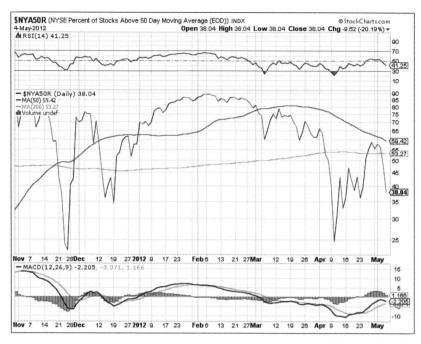

Figure 9.3 Percentage of stocks trading above the NYSE 50 day moving average

Source: StockCharts.com

That is how I use social mood. When I see examples of greater "us, everywhere, forever" behaviors, they enable me to confirm the health of rising markets. When I see examples of greater "me, here, now" behaviors, they enable me to confirm the weakness of falling markets. And when I see extremes in either pattern of behavior—particularly clustered patterns of behavior—I am on the watch for a potential turn in the markets. These patterns of behavior are the best indicators I know; and they keep the emotion out.

Too many investors I know spend their time focused entirely on the financial markets and specific company earnings and analyst reports. From my perspective, they are missing the forest for the trees. Changes in social mood cut across all aspects of our lives—from economics, politics, culture, the media, even the foods we eat. I strongly recommend that as you invest, you look broadly at the world around you for clues. Many of the reasons I saw a bottom looming in October 2011 and a peak on the horizon in February 2012 had nothing to do with the financial markets.

Final Thoughts

Whether one is long-term bullish or long-term bearish, I think it is important to recognize that social mood and our level of confidence move in series of concurrent cycles of differing degrees. That is to say, it is possible for a very long-term cycle to be negative and a shorter-term trend to be positive—and vice versa. For example, although the entire move from the Great Depression to 2000/2007 shows increasing levels of confidence, the period of the late 1960s and early 1970s was clearly a period of deteriorating social mood. Someone in 1966, for example, who believed that social mood could still become even stronger would ultimately be proven correct, but that person first would have had to experience a very painful almost 10 years.

I learned that lesson the hard way in 2009, before I was aware of socionomics. At that time I believed strongly that the financial crisis had not played all the way through, but I failed to grasp the idea that confidence could first move through a strong positive cycle—albeit shorter term. (As I write, the S&P 500 is up more than 100% since its March 2009 lows.) Because of the Horizon Preference framework, I can now clearly see the behavioral signs of self-assured uncertainty that I missed in 2009.

Today, although I continue to see signs of broad scale deterioration in mood that support my long-term bearish view, socionomics and the Horizon Preference framework enable me to also see when real-time behaviors suggest meaningful market tops and bottoms along the way. Rather than getting caught up in the emotion of volatile markets—or my own long-term view—I now focus on the behaviors I see around me and how those behaviors reflect mood.

I believe that better than any broker or analyst out there, the real-world patterns of behavior around us offer the best investment advice there is.

10

Final Thoughts

When Vince Lombardi said, "Confidence is contagious. And so is lack of confidence," I suspect that he didn't have the stock market at all in mind, but his quote fits the markets better than anything I have read from the financial pundits. Rising markets reflect growing confidence levels, whereas falling markets reveal the reverse.

The beauty of changing confidence, though, is how consistently it reveals itself in specific actions. We do the same things over and over based on our individual and collective levels of confidence without realizing it or knowing why. As confidence changes, our natural preferences change along with it. And the great news for investors is you can see it all in real time.

Hopefully the principles of socionomics that I have shared in this book, along with my Horizon Preference framework, will help you as an investor watch for the confidence-related behaviors around you and to see these behaviors for the true market indicators that they are. Even more, I hope it enables you to separate value-destroying emotion from your decisions to buy or sell a security.

The principles of socionomics and the Horizon Preference framework also apply to decision making well beyond the stock market. By understanding the direction of social mood and how it affects our natural choices, professionals in advertising, media, and product development can improve their effectiveness as well. For example, those who linked the natural "me, here, now" decision-making behaviors with falling confidence would have known that the rental industry would benefit enormously (and naturally) from the housing crisis.

And that is just one example. Recently, I asked a group of college students to look at the most successful television shows over the past 20 years and plot our level of confidence on a chart based on those shows. You'd be surprised how tightly their charts mirrored the S&P 500.

The students also told me that when their confidence was low, such as after a breakup, I could find them eating "comfort food," like a pint of Ben and Jerry's ice cream or mac and cheese, alone on the couch at home, in their pajamas, with their dog, listening to Adele. Without even realizing it, they had pulled together what sells in a "me, here, now" economy during a period of weak social mood.

When I was an adolescent, my father used to say, "Know where you are in time and space." At that particular time in my life, it was his way of telling me to straighten up. But he was right; our "when" and "where," and I'll add "who," matter—in business, in the markets, on television, at the movies, in voting booths, and even when, after a break up, we open our refrigerators and unknowingly choose "comfort food" for dinner.

Hopefully you now understand why.

Bibliography

Books

John Casti, *Mood Matters: From Rising Skirt Lengths to the Collapse of World Powers* (New York: Copernicus Books, 2010).

Constantin Malik, *Ahead of Change: How Crowd Psychology and Cybernetics Transform the Way We Govern* (Frankfurt: Campus Verlag, 2011).

Robert R. Prechter, Jr., *The Wave Principle of Human Social Behavior and the New Science of Socionomics* (Gainesville, GA: New Classics Library, 1999).

Robert R. Prechter, Jr., *Pioneering Studies in Socionomics* (Gainesville, GA: New Classics Library, 2003).

DVDs and Videos

David Edmond Moore, *History's Hidden Engine*. (Atlanta: EyeKiss Films, 2006), www.socionomics.net/hhe-part-1/.

Robert Prechter, *Toward a New Science of Social Prediction: Robert Prechter at the London School of Economics* (Gainesville, GA: Socionomics Institute, 2009).

The 2011 Socionomics Summit: New Horizons in the Study of Social Mood (Gainesville, GA: Socionomics Institute, 2011).

The 2012 Socionomics Summit: The Social Mood Conference (Gainesville, GA: Socionomics Institute, 2012), www.socionomicssummit.com/the-2012-social-mood-conference-on-demand/.

Online Resources

www.socionomics.net

www.horizonpreference.com

Papers

Johan Bollen, Huina Mao, and Xiaojun Zeng, "Twitter Mood Predicts the Stock Market," *Journal of Computational Science* 2, no. 1 (March 2011): 1–8.

John Nofsinger, "Social Mood and Financial Economics," *Journal of Behavioral Finance* 6, no. 3 (September 2005): 144–160.

Kenneth Olson, "A Literature Review of Social Mood," *Journal of Behavioral Finance* 7, no. 4 (December 2006): 193–203.

Robert R. Prechter, Jr. and Wayne D. Parker, "The Finan-cial/Economic Dichotomy in Social Behavioral Dynamics: The Socionomic Perspective," *Journal of Behavioral Finance* 8, no. 2 (June 2007): 84–108.

Robert R. Prechter, Jr., Deepak Goel, Wayne D. Parker, and Matthew Lampert, "Social Mood, Stock Market Perfor-mance and U.S. Presidential Elections: A Socionomic Per-spective on Voting Results" (February 2012), Social Science Research Network website, http://papers.ssrn.com/sol3/papers.cfm?abstract_id=1987160.

Subscriptions

The Socionomist, Gainesville, GA: Socionomics Institute. www.socionomics.net/socionomist-announcement/.

Index

Numbers

A

B

U

UBS, 111
"us, everywhere, forever," 151
utility value, 74

V

Vietnam, 112

W-X

The Wall Street Journal, 29
   Heard on the Street Column, 155
wars, market bottoms, 110
wealth effect, 41-42
   housing, 76
Wells Fargo, 18-20

Y-Z

year-end stock market valuation
   1927-2011, 148
year-end stock market valuation
   2000-2008, 147

DATE DUE
